I0167684

The Beak

Sherri Bee

South Island
Adventures

Copyright © 2023 Sherri Bee Ltd

Published by Sherri Bee Ltd, New Zealand
www.sherribee.com

Interior illustrations by Sherri Bee
Cover art by Angela Bradley
www.angelabradley.co.nz

All rights reserved. No part of this publication may be
reproduced or transmitted in any form by any means, electronic,
mechanical, digital, photocopying, recording or otherwise, or
stored in a retrieval system, without the written permission of the
copyright owner.

ISBN: 978-0-473-66558-6

Disclaimer: The characters and events in this book are entirely
fictitious and any resemblance to any person, living or dead, or any
event is purely coincidental.

For Nicola and Laura, who also dabbled in the world of bird-keeping.

Also by this author

The Glint

CONTENTS

Chapter 1: Mysterious Looks

Thirteen-year-old Talia Peterson yawned as she walked into the kitchen. Sitting down at the table with her plate of cereal, she glanced out the window. It was late November, and a beautiful summer morning. White petals of daisies stretched open as they drank in the early sunshine. Across the lake, on the distant mountains, there was just a little snow lingering along the high ridges.

Talia's mother came into the kitchen. She had a faraway look in her eyes as she headed for the coffee machine.

"Morning, Mum!" said Talia cheerfully.

Her mother jumped, startled. "Oh, morning, pet," she responded. The faraway look returned to her eyes.

Talia was familiar with this mood. She watched her mother covertly as the latter leaned back against the kitchen bench, while the machine poured the brown liquid into a cup. The machine stopped but her mother didn't move. She appeared to be gazing into another world.

Talia got up to take her dishes to the dishwasher. Mrs. Peterson moved aside automatically to make room for her to open it. "Thanks," said Talia. "Are you going to drink your coffee, Mum?"

Mrs. Peterson came back to herself with another jolt and picked up her cup. Sitting down at the table, she took a sip then put the cup on the table and gazed at Talia.

Talia giggled. "Wassup, Mum?" she asked.

Her mother looked at her speculatively for a moment, then said, "School holidays start soon, don't they?"

"Yup," said Talia. "Three weeks away. I can't wait."

"Hmm," murmured her mother. She continued to look at Talia.

"Why?" asked Talia. "Is something happening?"

"Maybe," said her mother mysteriously. She picked up her cup of coffee and moved towards the hallway. Turning back, she said brightly, "Have a good day at school, pet."

"Thanks, Mum. You, too. Oops, I mean have a good day working in your office." Talia giggled again.

Just then, her father came into the kitchen.

"Morning, pet!" he said, ruffling Talia's dark blonde hair.

"Oh, now I have to brush my hair again, Dad!" said Talia. "Morning!" She rummaged around in the pantry looking for something tasty to include in her school lunch. When she turned around again, it was to find her father

2

watching her with the same speculative gaze that her mother had.

"Not you, too, Dad!" she laughed. "Are Mum's deep looks catching?"

"Maybe," he answered, just as mysteriously as Mrs. Peterson. Changing the subject, he said, "Are you nearly ready to go to school? I need to get moving earlier today."

"I just need a few more minutes," said Talia. She hurried to finish putting her lunch together then went to the bathroom to brush her teeth and redo her hair.

At school, Talia found her good friends, Cassia and Belinda, also aged thirteen, waiting at the gate. They walked to their classroom together.

"Only three weeks of school left!" said Belinda, who was sometimes called Lindy.

"Yep," said Cassia. "And Christmas only a few weeks away!"

"Are your families going away anywhere?" asked Belinda wistfully. Belinda's mother, a single parent, was not able to take her two daughters away on holiday very often.

"Not that I know of," answered Cassia.

"Me neither," said Talia. "I'm wondering if something's up though," she added. "Mum and Dad were giving me weird looks this morning. Nothing strange about Mum doing that, but Dad was doing it, too!"

"Ooh, sounds intriguing," grinned Belinda. "The Case of the Mysterious Parents! Must have something to do with Christmas, surely."

"Guess I'll find out," said Talia.

The school bell went just then, so they separated and went to their desks.

After school, the three girls were joined by Cassia's older brother Cameron, known as Cam, and his best friend Mish, whose real name was Jason.

"Was Rick at school today?" asked Cassia, referring to Mish's eleven-year-old younger brother.

"I think I remember being followed by something," said Mish lightly. "I guess it could have been him."

Cassia rolled her eyes. It was hard to get Mish to take anything seriously!

Cam said to Cassia, "Mish's parents might have to go away for a couple of weeks. To see his uncle in Canada."

"Oh," said Cassia, looking at Mish. "No chance of you and Rick going as well? You might get to see some snow for Christmas if you went!"

Mish shrugged. He eyed Rick who had just walked up to the group. The brothers had strawberry blonde hair like their mother, but Mish had green eyes while Rick's eyes were almost black. There was a mischievous look in Mish's eyes at that moment.

"We all went to Canada for Christmas when I was about seven," Mish said. "The only thing I really remember about it is seeing Rick fall out of my uncle's sled, headfirst into a snowbank. Just his little legs were sticking out."

The girls giggled and Rick gave his brother an annoyed

4

look. "How was I able to breathe then, if I was upside down in the snow?" he demanded.

Mish shrugged again. "I'm sure they have snorkels in Canada," he said in a surprised tone.

Cam laughed. "I guess you were only four when that happened, Rick. Do you remember going to Canada?"

"Not really," said Rick sadly. "I wish we could go again! But Dad says it's not gonna work out this time."

Cam turned to Cassia. "I thought I'd ask if Mish and Rick could stay with us while their folks are away," he said.

"That would be nice. Would Toto come?" she asked. Toto was the boys' little Jack Russell terrier.

Mish shook his head. "No. My cousin is going to look after him."

There was a toot behind them. The children turned to see a small red hatchback stopping nearby. It was Belinda's mother with Belinda's little sister, Jackie, in the back of the car. Jackie had only recently started school and Belinda could see that she did not look happy. Her mother rolled down her window and called out.

"Come on, Lindy! Jackie jammed her finger in a door as we were leaving her school. I need to get her home pronto."

"Ouch," said Belinda. "Okay, Mum, coming!" She turned to the others. "See you tomorrow, everyone!" Waving at her friends, she climbed into the car.

The rest of the group dispersed, making their way to their own homes.

Mysterious Looks

That evening, only half an hour after dinner, Talia's mother came into the lounge where Talia and her father were watching television. She settled herself comfortably next to her husband, as though she was going to watch with them. Talia stared at her in astonishment. Usually, her mother would still be hard at work in her office at this time of night. Mrs. Peterson jabbed her husband's knee then both parents looked over at Talia.

"What's going on?" asked Talia. "Why are you two being so mysterious?"

"Are we?" said her mother, looking surprised.

Mr. Peterson grinned. "Maybe we are," he said. "But your mother has an idea."

"What is it?" asked Talia. "Is it to do with Christmas?"

"No, it's not," answered Mrs. Peterson. "It's before that. I need to do some special research. It involves going to some kind of remote, sparsely populated location. Preferably somewhere no one else has ever really been to."

Talia was intrigued. "Where were you thinking?" she asked. "Does this mean Dad and I have to cook for ourselves again for a while?"

Her father answered. "No. We were thinking the location we have in mind would make a great camping holiday."

"Where, Dad?" Talia asked, her interest aroused.

"Down in one of the lesser travelled sounds on the southwest coast," he said.

"One can only get there by air or sea," added Mrs.

Peterson. "So, I was thinking we could charter a bigger boat to take us all there, be dropped off with all our camping gear, and be picked up about ten days later. Back just in time for Christmas."

Talia felt excited. "But why a bigger boat? What kind of gear are you taking?"

Mr. Peterson smiled. "Perhaps enough camping gear for six kids, one dog and two adults," he said. "We wondered if you and your friends would like to go camping together."

"Oooh, I'm sure they would love to!" exclaimed Talia. She felt thrilled. Camping in a place no one else had been to before! "Do you want me to ask them? It would be handy because Mish and Rick's parents are going to Canada soon, they said."

"I think in this instance I will do the asking," said Mrs. Peterson. "I take it you like the idea?"

"I love it!" said Talia enthusiastically. "When will you call them?"

"Probably tomorrow night," answered her mother. "So please don't say anything to your friends yet."

"I won't," promised Talia.

Chapter 2: Preparing for a Holiday

The next day at school, Talia couldn't stop thinking about the proposed camping trip. She hoped her friends' parents would let them go! Now and then she glanced at Cassia and Belinda speculatively.

After this had happened a few times Belinda said to her, "Talia, did you know you're giving us mysterious looks? Is that how your parents were looking at you? What are you thinking about?"

Talia giggled and looked at them innocently. "Was I?" She had no idea that both the other girls were thinking how much she looked like her mother at that moment.

"Come on, tell us," said Cassia, twirling her long dark hair around her finger. "We know there's something going on! You can't hide it from us!"

"There is something," said Talia, "but I can't say

anything about it yet, although I want to. I might be able to talk about it tomorrow."

"Okay," said Belinda. "We won't let you forget!"

"Oh, I don't think there's much chance of me forgetting," responded Talia, giving them another mysterious look. Her hazel eyes were dancing. She just hoped her parents wouldn't forget to ask the other parents!

They didn't. That night Mrs. Peterson herself rang around the other families and explained what she was doing. They all gave permission for their young ones to go on the camping trip.

Talia was sprawled out over the couch in the lounge, watching her favourite television show. She had become so engrossed in it that she had temporarily forgotten about going camping.

Her mother came into the lounge near the end of the show. "Well, that's settled!" she said cheerfully.

"What?" said Talia. "Oh! The trip! Yippee! Is everyone allowed to go?" She sat up straight, forgetting about the show, which was just coming up to its most suspenseful moment.

"Apparently!" said her mother.

Talia raced to the phone to call Belinda and Cassia. They were both excited, too.

"Cam said Mish and Rick are really happy about coming," Cassia told Talia over the phone. "They thought they were going to have to stay at their cousin's house — that one who has a bunch of noisy little kids that they sometimes have to share a room with."

"Ha, not much chance of them seeing any noisy little kids on this trip," said Talia. "Although we both know what Mish would say if he heard me say that!"

Cassia laughed. She knew Talia was referring to Mish's habitual teasing of Rick.

After Talia got off the phone, she remembered the television show and went back to the lounge. "What happened, Dad?" she asked her father. "Did they find out who left the black shoes in the boot?"

"Have no idea," he said. "What black shoes?"

"Aw, the black shoes on my TV show," said Talia. "I thought you were watching it, too. Dang."

The last three weeks of the school year seemed to go slowly. There were relaxed days when the students didn't do much except quizzes, games, sports or watch their choice of movie. Desks were cleaned out and artwork taken off walls. In the last week of all, prize-giving was held. Everyone clapped hard when Rick was awarded the prize for excellence over all the classes of his entire grade. Belinda and Cam also received prizes. On the last day of school, they all attended the final assembly for the year. Then the students were dismissed.

There was a happy clamour of shouting, laughing, Christmas well-wishing and goodbyes as everyone left the school grounds.

Talia was standing with Cassia and Belinda. She motioned to them to wait, then called Mish, Rick and Cam over as they came walking by.

"Hey guys! All ready to go on Monday?" she asked. "And are you all able to pop over to my place tomorrow after lunch to talk about final stuff for the trip?"

There was a happy clamour of shouting, laughing, Christmas well-wishing and goodbyes as everyone left the school grounds.

The others nodded. Rick said, "This is so awesome, Talia!"

His brother said, "Man, what other parents would want to take six kids camping! And a dog!"

"Yeah, I was surprised they said Clumpy could come," agreed Talia. Clumpy was a black Labrador, belonging to Cam and Cassia. "Mum said they had to get special written permission for him to come, because of the wildlife that might be around. I think he was only allowed 'cos they know he's not brave enough to chase anything."

Cam looked offended for a moment then he laughed. "I guess that's true," he said. "More likely to hide from a small animal than chase it! I think he missed out on the 'retrieving' part of being a Labrador. But I did hear Dad saying something about a dog being handy in case someone got lost."

"Well, hopefully that won't happen," remarked Belinda. "In case he doesn't want to retrieve us either! There's Mum – gotta go. See you tomorrow at Talia's house!" She waved and ran to her mother's car.

The next afternoon all six of them were crowded into the Petersons' lounge.

"Here's the brief," said Mrs. Peterson. "You need to make sure you have everything you need because once we're dropped off by the boat, we can't come back for anything. So, if you forget your pillow or your hairbrush, that'll just be tough luck for you."

"Yeah, Rick, don't you dare forget your hairbrush," said Mish to his younger brother. "Can't have you coming back looking like a wild man!"

Mrs. Peterson paused and looked at Rick. His strawberry blonde hair certainly did not look wild, as it was cut short and was quite straight. "I would be surprised if not having a hairbrush even made a difference to Rick's hair," she said.

Cam and Mish looked at each other and choked back a laugh. Rick ignored them. "Can we bring cell phones with us?" he asked Mrs. Peterson.

"There's not a lot of point," she answered, "unless you have a camera on your phone. But there won't be anywhere you can charge the phones. Some kind of camera would be good, though. It might be a great place to get some nature photos, or even if you want to take pictures of each other. If Mish forgets to take *his* hairbrush, for instance." She looked down at the list she was holding. Mish looked taken aback and Rick smirked at him, grinning to himself and thinking what a cool lady Talia's mother was.

"What tents do you have?" asked Mr. Peterson.

Cam answered. "Mum and Dad are letting us bring their big two room tent."

"I was hoping Talia, Lindy and I could use that one," said Cassia. "Unless the adults need it?" she added.

"Nope, we have our own big tent," said Talia's mother. "You girls can use that one. What are you boys doing then?" she asked, turning to them.

"Mish and I are going to use his blue dome tent and Rick has his own even smaller tent," said Cam.

"Clumpy might have to share that tent. To save Rick from all the wild animals," added Mish.

Rick snorted. "More likely I will have to protect Clumpy from wild animals! Even like a sparrow."

"Hey, don't insult my dog," protested Cam, but Cassia

was laughing.

"You know Rick is probably right," she told her brother.

"Back to business," said Mrs. Peterson. "Do you all have warm sleeping bags? It can get pretty cold at night in the sounds. And pack warm clothes."

"But it's summer now, Mum," protested Talia. "Don't you think we'll get hot? I'm gonna bring my togs."

"Yes, well, you can bring swimming things and light clothing but make sure you pack warm clothing as well," emphasized her mother. "The weather can change suddenly there."

Everyone felt excited again. Camping and swimming in the middle of nowhere! Unpredictable weather!

"Why do they call them 'sounds'?" asked Cassia.

"Technically, they're not sounds," responded Mrs. Peterson. "They're fjords, spelled f-j-o-r-d but pronounced 'fee-yord'. It can also be spelled f-i-o-r-d. Fjords are formed by glaciers – deep valleys, filled with water, that have been carved out over a very long time. Sounds are usually rivers that have been flooded a good distance inland, forming inlets. Sometimes the two words get used interchangeably, though. Where we are going there are a lot of very deep fjords. Not many people have been to most of them!"

"This really is a wonderful opportunity for us all," added her husband. "You may never get another chance like this. Make the most of it!"

"Wow," said Rick in awe.

"Thanks so much for letting us come," added Cam.

They finished discussing the details of the gear they were to take, then had afternoon tea. Talia had made hot scones with jam and cream for everyone.

"Better enjoy those," said Mr. Peterson. "Won't be anything like that where we're going!"

"What other food do we need to bring?" asked Belinda.

"Don't worry about that; our parents have sorted all the food between them," put in Cassia quickly. "There'll be plenty!"

"If not, you can catch and skin a rabbit," suggested Mish.

Cassia and Belinda looked horrified. Talia and Rick rolled their eyes and Cam chuckled.

"Actually, I will be interested to see how many rabbits there *are*," said Mrs. Peterson. "They sure are a pest in other areas of the country, but I don't know how many we will see down there. Great scones, pet. Do any of you mind if I have that last one?" She reached out and grabbed the remaining scone before anyone answered.

"I guess no one minds," grinned Mish.

Chapter 3: Up the Coast

The day of departure finally arrived. The Petersons had chartered a fishing vessel. It would take them up the coast and into the seldom travelled sound where they were going to camp. They had also hired a large van to drive everyone to the port where they would board.

During the drive, the children chattered merrily as the countryside raced past beside them. Clumpy lay on the floor beneath Cam's legs, tongue hanging out. He was enjoying himself, too, his eyes moving from person to person as they spoke. Occasionally Cam reached down to pat his head and Clumpy licked his hand.

It took a couple of hours to reach the port. Once they arrived, the children were allowed to buy themselves some lunch from a café as a treat, since it would be a while before they saw a shop again. It was a little chilly in the coastal town, so they all opted for hot food. Then they walked back to the wharf where Mr. and Mrs. Peterson were overseeing the loading of everything onto the fishing boat. It had a roomy cabin built along the centre of its deck, with a small wheelhouse in front, above some amenity areas, and there was a hold for storage and an engine room below deck. Fishing crates and other gear were securely stacked at the sides of the vessel.

Talia had bought some hot food for her parents also, and now she took it over to them along with the hot drinks they had asked for. They took it off her gratefully. "Wow, Dad, is this the boat we're going on?" she asked him – somewhat unnecessarily, as it was clear that was where their tents and other belongings were being stowed!

Her father nodded, taking a bite of his hot dog. "When you kids have finished eating, we'll get you all over here and introduce you to the skipper and his crew. Then you might all want to use a real bathroom for the last time for a while before we get going."

Talia went back to the others and updated them.

"A real bathroom?" queried Belinda. "Is it going to be that bad where we're going then?"

Mish grinned at her. "Haven't you ever been camping before?" he asked. "It's hole-digging time. And no showers."

Cassia looked surprised. "I hope there'll be somewhere we can wash!" she said.

Talia laughed. "I think we're taking a portable loo," she

17

said. "But someone will probably have to empty it every day," she added mischievously.

They finished up their food then all of them used the local public restrooms as suggested. By that time, Talia's parents were looking for them, yelling to them all to hurry up. They hurried, running over to the wharf.

"Do you need a hand with loading anything?" asked Cam, as he looked at the empty van guiltily.

Mrs. Peterson laughed. "I think it's a bit late for that," she said. "But don't worry, you'll have plenty to do once we get there." She winked.

Just then the skipper appeared, along with his two crew members. Mrs. Peterson introduced each of the children to the crew by name then said, "Kids, this is Captain Rodney, and these are Kotiri and Fahey." She gestured towards the men.

Captain Rodney greeted the children and said, "You can all call me Rod. And that's not as in 'fishing rod' in case you thought that! I get asked that all the time." The children laughed.

"Gotcha, Rod," said Mish.

Cassia spoke up shyly. "Have you met our dog, Clumpy, Captain Rod? Here, Clumpy, say hello to the ship's captain!"

The captain jumped back as if stung, looking terrified. "A dog!" he exclaimed. "When did this happen? I'll have to charge you double price or else throw him overboard."

The three girls and Rick looked shocked. Talia looked

towards her parents with wide eyes. They didn't seem concerned. Mr. Peterson laughed and walked away to give the keys of the van to the person from the local hire depot, who had just arrived to collect it.

Mish caught the twinkle in the captain's eyes. "Okay, sir, I think you got us on that one," said Mish.

Cassia loosened her grip on Clumpy's collar. She hadn't even realized how tightly she was holding it. She saw now that the captain and Talia's mother were laughing. So was Cam.

Clumpy chose that moment to leap from the wharf to the boat. "Well, he wasn't fooled, eh," commented Kotiri, the slightly shorter of the two crew members.

"I'm really surprised he jumped on board so fast!" exclaimed Cam. "Boats aren't usually his thing." Suddenly Clumpy appeared from around a corner with something in his mouth. "Oh, no, he's got someone's fish! NO, Clumpy!"

Cassia looked towards the captain nervously. He laughed. "Looks like he found a bit of bait. There was some sitting in a bucket. It won't hurt him."

Despite the reassurance, Cam took the bait away from the dog and got him settled in a warm corner on an old cushion while everyone else climbed on board. There was plenty of room for them all. The crew untied the ropes from the moorings and the vessel chugged slowly away from the pier.

"How long will it take us to get there?" Cam asked the

captain.

"As long as we don't meet any storms, should be a few hours," he responded.

Cassia and Belinda looked at each other uncertainly. They didn't quite know what to make of this captain. Talia laughed. She had spent quite a lot of time on boats with her parents.

"Don't worry, girls," she smiled. "The captain would have had to check the forecast and if there were any storms on the way we probably wouldn't be going today."

"If one *does* pop up, I bet even he didn't know about it," joked Mish.

Captain Rod grinned at him. "That'd be right," he agreed. "But it looks like fair weather today. Might be a little choppy as we go around the bluff."

Once they reached the open sea, the captain increased speed. Fahey took over the steering wheel and Captain Rod disappeared below into the engine compartment. Kotiri stayed with the passengers, who were seated on the side of the deck facing the land, pointing out wildlife and interesting land features as they passed them.

"See that seal colony?" he asked. Everyone craned their necks to look where he was pointing at the coastal rocks.

"I wouldn't have even noticed them if you hadn't said anything!" exclaimed Cassia. "They just about blend right in; they are the same grey as the rocks."

Kotiri nodded. Fahey gave a shout from the wheelhouse. "Get to the front everyone!" They all jumped up and ran as close to the bow as they could get.

"Dolphins!" shouted Rick in excitement. They watched, entranced, as the graceful creatures divided into a stream on each side of the boat, now and then leaping into the air and diving into the water again. Their very eyes seemed happy and joyful. The dolphins accompanied them along the coast for several kilometres before finally changing their course, heading out to sea.

They watched, entranced, as the graceful creatures divided into a stream on each side of the boat, now and then leaping into the air and diving into the water again.

Belinda sighed with pleasure. "Wow. That was so awesome," she said. "It was worth coming just to see the dolphins. Jackie and Mum would have loved those!"

"I got some video footage on my phone," said Mish. "You can show them when we're back."

"Cool, thanks!" said Belinda.

Up the Coast

By now they were heading around the bluff, at the southwest of the country, beginning to turn north. The sea became a bit rough, as the captain had predicted. Everyone gripped their seats or the side of the boat as it heaved up and down on the swells.

The strong sea breeze caused Belinda's long blonde hair to keep blowing into her face and eyes. Finally, she said to the other girls, "Do you have a hair tie? I should have tied my hair up."

Cassia and Talia shook their heads, but Mrs. Peterson overheard and produced a rubber band from her pocket. "Maybe this'll help," she said, passing it to Belinda, who took it gratefully, pulling her hair into a somewhat untidy ponytail.

Cam turned to make a comment to Mish, and to his surprise, saw that Mish was looking rather green. "What's the matter, bud?" said Cam.

Mish tried to smile. "Never been on a ship out on the open sea," he said. "Even a small one like this. Rick, are you okay?"

His younger brother was looking equally green. "Uh – no," said Rick, before suddenly rushing to lean over the side, holding onto his glasses tightly as he did so. A few seconds later Mish joined him.

The others looked on sympathetically. Mish stood up straight, looking embarrassed. "Never thought I'd be the seasick type!" he said. "The sea is a bit different to the lake, isn't it?"

Mr. Peterson chuckled. "Can be a lot moodier," he said.

Cassia got some tissues for the boys so they could wipe their chins and mouths. The brothers sat down, both still looking somewhat off colour.

"None of the boat trips across the lake were as rough as this when we were looking for the cause of the glint," said Mish, referring to the wonderful adventure that had happened much earlier in the year.

Fahey poked his head out of the wheelhouse and grinned down at them. "You'll find it gets a bit calmer for the rest of the trip," he said. "And once we're into the fjord, it'll be calmer than my grandmother."

Talia giggled. "Is your grandmother pretty grumpy then, Fahey?"

Fahey rubbed his black moustache and sighed sadly. "I have to keep 'er in order," he said. "It's not so bad now she's no longer with us."

"Did she move away?" asked Belinda with interest.

"Nup," said Fahey. "Lying yonder, next to me Great-Uncle Bob." He gestured towards the distant shores, then turned back to the steering wheel.

Mish wanted to laugh but had to rush to the side of the boat again. "Just great," he muttered.

However, true to Fahey's word, the sea did become smoother as they headed up the side of the coast. The two brothers' stomachs began to settle down and they were able to enjoy the scenery with the others, passing fascinating looking islands with overhanging, cathedral-like arches. Hundreds of sea birds floated in the air on the updraughts beside the high cliff faces.

Finally, after passing by several fjord openings, Fahey turned the vessel towards the land. The captain reappeared on deck and relieved Fahey at the steering wheel. Rick and Mish eyed the white caps at the mouth of the approaching sound nervously. Kotiri, who had taken a liking to Clumpy and was giving him a pat, noticed their anxious glances.

"Won't be a problem," he said to them. "There's a bit of a sand bar at the mouth of this sound, but it doesn't go all the way across. There's a narrow channel that we can go through."

Belinda exclaimed. "Look! The dolphins are back!"

Kotiri looked over the side at the beautiful mammals. "Naw, different, these are," he said. "Bottle-nosed."

The six young people and Mr. and Mrs. Peterson leaned over the side.

"These dolphins are bigger than the other ones," commented Mr. Peterson.

Mish handed his cell phone to Cam. "Can you video record them, please, Cam?" he asked. "I still feel a bit queasy."

Cam nodded and filmed the dolphins, which continued to swim alongside them right through the break in the sand bar into the sound. Then the dolphins did a few leaps into the air and turned back to return to the open sea.

"Almost as if they were saying goodbye," commented Cassia, and Talia and Belinda agreed.

Chapter 4: Inside the Fjord

Once they had traversed the sand bar and were right inside the fjord, the sea became completely flat. Tall mountains rose starkly on either side of them as the vessel moved through the narrow entrance. Apart from the sound of the chugging engine, it was very quiet. All the passengers looked up with awe at the sheer, steep cliffs. Soon the fjord widened, and they could see vegetation growing over and around the bottom of the mountains. The land was becoming less steep, too.

Talia asked her mother, "Do you already know where we're going to camp, Mum? Doesn't seem like much flat land around here."

"I had a good look over the maps before we decided which sound to come into," her mother answered. "I expect to find some more open areas further in, alongside a stream that opens into the sound."

The captain took the fishing vessel further into the fjord, eventually coming to an intersection of three smaller waterways. Mrs. Peterson directed him to steer towards the one at the far right. The land on either side of this smaller branch of the fjord was much closer to sea level, with a lot of native trees and plants. They passed some more seals sunning themselves on rocky outcrops. The seals raised their heads and watched the passers-by with curiosity but remained where they were.

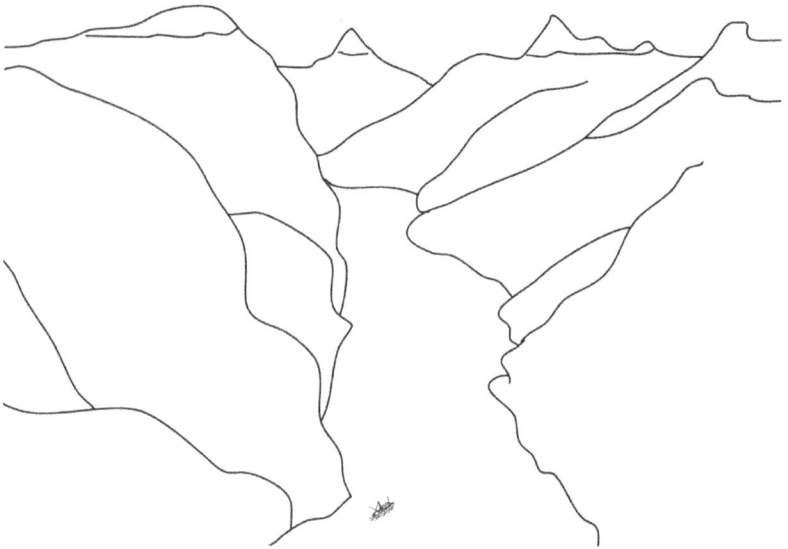

Tall mountains rose starkly on either side of them as the vessel moved through the narrow entrance.

The Beak

"They don't seem worried about us being here," commented Belinda.

"I guess they don't see people very often, if at all," said Mrs. Peterson. She was watching the passing vegetation closely, looking for anything relating to her research as well as the small stream that she had seen on the map.

Everyone on the boat, including the crew, was having a good look around as they travelled deeper into the sound. The land looked completely untouched, as though no one had ever been there! No huts, no sign of any man-made object. Fahey and Kotiri chatted a bit about potentially good fishing spots. Cam and Mish listened to their conversation with interest. They and Mr. Peterson had all brought fishing rods. Rick's eyes scoured the sides of the mountains, hoping to see a glint of gold poking out somewhere!

Finally, Mrs. Peterson called out. "Okay, there it is, I think! That opening over there – see the stream emptying into the sound?"

Captain Rodney looked over to where she was pointing and carefully maneuvred the large boat in that direction. Fortunately, there were some huge flat rocks that appeared to have straight perpendicular sides only a few metres away from the stream. He checked the instrumentation on the boat's console. One of these was able to detect objects underwater nearby. He allowed the children to have a look at what he was doing, and they noted the shapes that showed up as the boat neared them. There were some rocks just out of sight under the surface to one side of the straight rocks, but the captain was able to turn the boat around and reverse slowly into a narrow space right up against a wide, flat rock.

"Almost like it was made for us," commented Cam.

"That's handy," said Mr. Peterson. "Now we won't have to use the dinghy to transport everything to land in multiple trips. We can pass it all straight off the ship to someone on land." There was a small dinghy hanging on the side of the central cabin.

Mrs. Peterson called the children to attention. "Okay, everyone," she said. "Now is the time for some real work! But first I need to go for a wee scout and see if I can find a suitable place to put up the tents." She did expect to find a spot, as the map had shown flat contours on the land around the area. "You may as well all come with me."

Mish and Rick were very glad to get off the boat. They clambered out with the others and Clumpy leaped off as well. But he landed on a slippery part of the rock and slid down into the water with a splash.

"Clumpy!" exclaimed Cassia in fright. But the big dog didn't seem worried in the least. He dog paddled happily past the rock to a little beach area covered in pebbles. Dragging himself out of the water, he had a shake then went to the nearest tree.

Meanwhile, Talia's parents and all the youngsters had got off the boat and were now walking towards the stream. Clumpy raced to catch up with them. The vegetation was

28

quite sparse just there, so there was enough room on one side of the stream for all of them to walk alongside it as they followed it upstream.

Only a short distance inland, the trees opened out into an area with short grass and tussock. The stream became wider and deeper. They could see that it extended quite some way into the tussock that was further afield.

"Wow, that tussock looks like it goes for miles," commented Belinda. "What a vast space!" she added, as they gazed out over the distant tussock.

Cassia shivered. "It does look untouched," she said. "Makes me feel kind of weird. Have we gone back in time?"

Mrs. Peterson looked amused. "I think this will be a great spot to set up the tents," she said. "Pretty flat, with water nearby, and a few trees just over there. What do you all think?"

Talia said, "I think it's an awesome place to camp!" The others nodded in agreement.

"What do you think, Clumpy?" Cassia asked the dog. He wagged his tail and got up to come to her, but quickly lay down when there was a sudden whoosh and a loud caw as a bird swooped over them, coming very close to Clumpy's head. He looked up in astonishment.

Rick laughed. "It's a kea!" he said.

"How fun!" said Talia. "There'll probably be a few of them then! We'd better watch our stuff. They like chewing things."

"Yes, cheeky birds," said her father. "Well, let's get back to the boat and get all our stuff so that the crew can return to the port. And we need to get the tents up before dark – it's midafternoon now."

The children nodded and began to make their way back to the shore where the crew was still waiting.

It took several trips of carrying gear back and forth from the shore to the camping site but finally it was done. Then everyone went back to the fishing boat one more time to say goodbye to the crew.

Cassia was about to thank the captain when she paused. She thought she had heard an odd sound that seemed quite close. "Did any of you hear that?" she asked everyone.

"Hear what?" said Talia. "I can only hear the water lapping and the sound of the boat engine. It's really quiet around here!"

"I can't quite describe it," said Cassia. "Was maybe like someone in pain."

"Really," said Fahey thoughtfully. "Well, best watch out for bears."

Cassia was startled. "I didn't think we had bears in this country!"

'We don't," said Mrs. Peterson firmly. "Except for those in a zoo. Fahey is pulling your leg. It was probably just a bird. Maybe even the kea we saw."

Cassia nodded and put the sound out of her mind. She knew it didn't sound like a bear!

Captain Rod laughed. "Who knows what's out there,"

he said mischievously. "Well, we'll see you when we come back, if the wild bears haven't got you!" He grinned then headed for the wheelhouse.

Fahey untied the rope that had been slung around a tall rock to stop the vessel from drifting away. He and Kotiri exchanged a final goodbye with the campers before waving and also turning towards the wheelhouse.

Belinda felt strange as she watched the now familiar craft move away and pick up speed as it headed back out into deeper water. Now they were really on their own! The other girls were already walking towards the stream. Belinda followed them and soon they were back in the open tussock area.

Chapter 5: Setting Up Camp

Mr. Peterson called the three girls over to him. "Here's your big tent, Cassia," he said. "Looks like a good site over there," he added, gesturing to a grassy area not far from the nearby trees.

Cassia grabbed the tent bag. Belinda and Talia quickly came to help and the three of them lugged it over to their spot.

Rick had found his little tent and was busily pulling its components out of its bag. Cam and Mish were still looking for a good spot for their dome tent. They finally settled on an area a bit further away, with a backdrop of some thick bushes to provide a bit of shelter from the wind, and began putting up the tent. Rick took his tent over to them.

"Can you help me, please, Mish?" he asked his brother.

"When I'm done with ours," Mish answered. "Have you chosen a spot? Not too close to us. We don't want to be kept awake by your snoring!"

"Clumpy sometimes snores," said Cam with a grin.

"Maybe he and Rick should share the same tent then," retorted Mish, as he hoisted the flexible tent poles into position inside the blue canvas.

"I don't mind if Clumpy shares my tent," said Rick. "But I don't snore anyway. I like these bushes – think I'll put mine just over here." He walked a metre or two away from them.

"That's too close!" protested Mish. He picked up Rick's bundle of tent gear and moved it a bit further away. "How about here!"

Rick shrugged. "Okay. But I need some help. Can I help with yours?"

"I think we're all good, Rick," Cam told him. "I'll come give you a hand with yours soon."

Cam finished tightening the ropes on the tent pegs in the ground, walking around the dome tent to make sure he hadn't missed any.

Then both the older boys grabbed items for Rick's tent and within a short time it was up, canvas door flapping open in the gentle breeze. Rick thanked them gratefully. "I'll try my best not to snore too loudly," he joked.

Talia's parents had set up their own large tent some distance away from all the young people. Theirs had a big front awning that they were going to use as the eating area.

Mr. Peterson had also found a private nook between some trees not too far away and had set up the specially shaped upright tent for the portable toilet.

By the time all the tents were up, mattresses inflated, sleeping bags laid out and personal belongings stashed inside the tents, everyone was hot, thirsty and hungry. Biscuits and fruit juice were supplied while they were on the boat, but that seemed like a long time ago now.

Mr. Peterson got out the gas stove they were going to use and showed all the children how to get it going safely, so that they could boil water from the stream and heat up food. He had also brought some battery-powered lanterns, and of course, everyone had torches. As the sun went down, they turned on the lanterns and there was a cheerful glow of soft light around the campsite, attracting some curious insects.

Talia, who enjoyed both camping and cooking, offered to prepare the first evening's meal for everyone. Cassia and Belinda helped, giving Mrs. Peterson the chance to go for a walk beyond the campsite before it got completely dark. She was eager to begin her research the next morning.

Clumpy was having an interesting time. The kea had returned with a couple of its friends, and Clumpy attempted to creep up on the birds with the intention of barking at them. But when one of the birds turned to give him a peck and a scolding, the dog yelped and ran for the cover of Cam's tent.

"I think Clumpy will want to sleep in your tent tonight,"

Rick said to Cam.

"Will you be okay on your own, Rick?" asked Mrs. Peterson, overhearing this as she reappeared between some bushes. She was carrying leaves of some kind.

"Yep, thanks," said Rick, smiling. "Cam said Clumpy snores, so they will be awake all night while I get to snooze. If anything tries to get us in the night, it will hear them first."

Mrs. Peterson laughed. She went over to the eating area where the girls were just beginning to serve dinner into camp dishes.

"Dinner's ready!" called Belinda.

Everyone hurried over eagerly. There were canvas camping chairs for everyone to sit on. The three girls had prepared beans and curried sausages, and there was buttered bread for each person to wipe up the remains of the sauce on their plates.

"Yummy," said Mr. Peterson. "Thanks for making dinner, girls! Boys, it'll be your turn tomorrow night."

Cam nodded. He quite enjoyed cooking and had already peeked at the food supplies to see what was available. Now he said, "I reckon we'll come up with something fantastic. Eh, Mish and Rick?"

"But of course!" agreed Mish. "And Rick can be our gopher – we'll get him to do the fetching and carrying." He grinned at Rick who grinned back, nodding.

"I'd rather do that than cook," said Rick.

Cam turned to the adults. "Where are we storing all the

cold stuff?" he asked.

"There's a good little spot just over there in the stream," answered Mrs. Peterson. "We've put the whole chilly bin in it. The water here is so cold that it will refrigerate everything nicely."

"How cool," said Cassia.

"Literally," agreed Mish with an innocent look.

"Mum, did you see anything interesting for your project when you went for a walk before?" asked Talia.

"Yes, I did," said her mother. "Also, if you lot want to do a bit of exploring, I suspect there may be another stream not too far away. Perhaps with rapids. I thought I could hear a bit of a rushing water sound."

The young people were intrigued to hear this. They all made up their minds to go exploring the next day to find the rushing water.

By this time, everyone was feeling tired. After clearing the dinner dishes away, they all opted to go to their tents. The girls decided to have a quick game of cards in their shared tent, and Mish and Cam asked Rick if he would like to do the same with them in their dome tent.

Rick thought of his comfy looking sleeping bag on his air mattress and yawned. "No, thanks," he said. "I'm going to bed. Goodnight, everyone!" The others called out their own goodnights as Rick crawled into his little tent and zipped up the door flap.

Within an hour everyone else had done the same; lamps were turned off and the little campsite became silent and dark. As Rick had predicted, Clumpy had pushed his way into Cam's tent and was lying on one of Cam's jerseys, sound asleep. It had been a big day for him, too!

Chapter 6: An Odd Shadow

Nearly everyone slept soundly that night. Clumpy didn't even snore. Mrs. Peterson woke shortly after midnight feeling as though she had forgotten something very important. After tossing and turning for a while, she got up, turned on her big torch and searched through the case of paperwork she had brought. She made such a loud rustling sound that it woke her husband.

"What are you doing?" he asked patiently. He was used to this kind of thing from his wife.

"Did you see that booklet on native flora somewhere?" she responded. "I just need to check something."

Mr. Peterson leaned over and picked up the booklet in question from the floor, where it was nestled between a couple of maps. "This one?" he said.

Mrs. Peterson looked sheepish. "Oh, yes, sorry," she

said. "Now we can get back to sleep!"

Her husband rolled his eyes and turned over, snuggling back down into his sleeping bag. Mrs. Peterson flipped through the booklet to the page she wanted to look at. "Ah," she said quietly. She found a piece of paper to use as a bookmark and placed it in the booklet. Then she crawled quietly back into her own sleeping bag and fell asleep again.

Early the next morning, Cam was the first to wake. He felt as though he was being squashed. He opened one eye sleepily to find Clumpy taking up half the space on his sleeping bag. The dog was awake and seemed fidgety, whining a little and trying to get closer to him. Cam pushed Clumpy gently off his mattress, glancing towards the door as he did so. Then he gave a start. In the dim morning light, he thought he could see a shadow outside the tent. It was at least as tall as the tent.

Propping himself up on one elbow, Cam opened his eyes properly to get a better look. Yes, there was something outside the door. It reminded him of a very tall bird! He was sure he could see the shape of a beak. Meanwhile, Clumpy was still whining.

Cam looked over at Mish. The only part of him that was visible was a thatch of strawberry blonde hair, flopping over a pillow that was almost completely engulfed by his sleeping bag.

"Mish!" Cam whispered. There was no answer. "Mish!" Cam said again, more loudly. The only response was a grunt from the depths of the sleeping bag.

Cam looked back towards the shadow. It was gone. He crawled out of his sleeping bag, causing Clumpy, who was trying to get back on the mattress, to fall off onto the tent floor. Cam unzipped the door of the tent. Poking his head outside, he looked around. There was nothing there except tussock and the nearby bushes.

In the dim morning light, he thought he could see a shadow outside the tent.

"That was weird," thought Cam. Since he was awake, he decided to use the portable toilet, having a good look around as he walked over to the trees where it was located. Everything was very quiet. He couldn't even hear any birds just then.

The Beak

As he returned to his tent, Talia's parents emerged from theirs. "Morning, Cam!" they both said. He greeted them with a smile.

It wasn't long before everyone was awake and there was happy chatter as people washed at the stream and organized breakfast. Two kea birds also arrived and strode around the kitchen area looking for tidbits. They didn't appear frightened at all by the intruders.

As they ate their cereal, Cam mentioned what he had seen to the other children. "There was something outside my tent this morning," he said. "Clumpy was quite bothered by it."

"What was it?" asked Belinda.

"And why didn't you wake me?" asked Mish, pretending to be offended.

"I did try to wake you," said Cam with a grin. "You were totally out to it and when I looked back, it was gone."

"What was gone?" asked Rick, pushing his glasses up his nose. "My tent is close to yours. I didn't see anything."

"It was a big shadow of something moving," said Cam. "Like a tall bird."

Mish laughed. "What made it look like a bird?" he asked teasingly. "Did it squawk?" Mish flapped his arms up and down, squawking like a chicken.

Cam threw a twig at him. "It didn't make any sound," he said. "But it looked like it had a beak."

Talia looked at Cassia and Belinda. "Maybe it will come visit us tomorrow morning," she suggested.

An Odd Shadow

Cassia looked doubtful. "Not sure that I want mysterious shadows hanging out at our tent. What if it was something else – or someone else?"

"Ooh!" said Talia. "What if?"

Belinda screwed up her eyes. "Maybe it was nothing," she said. "Maybe Cam was just having a nightmare."

Cam snorted at this. "I was awake. Just ask Clumpy."

Cassia giggled and looked at Clumpy, who was crunching on dog biscuits. "Is it true, Clumpy? Was there something outside your tent this morning?"

The Labrador looked at her happily and kept crunching. One of the kea chose that moment to dart forward and steal a piece of dog biscuit. Clumpy leaped up to get the biscuit back but the green-feathered bird quickly flew away with its prize, cackling in triumph. It landed on a branch next to its companion, who immediately grabbed the stolen bit of dog biscuit with its hooked beak and swallowed it. The first kea rose up into the air, flapping around in circles and squawking angrily.

The children watched all this with amusement. "Serves it right!" laughed Rick. "What a thief!"

"If there was something outside your tent, Cam, Clumpy doesn't seem worried about it now," commented Belinda, returning to their conversation. "Wonder if it will come back again! If there was anything at all."

"Maybe it was just a shadow from a tree," offered Rick. "A little branch on a tree might look like a beak if its shadow could be seen through the tent."

"I didn't think any of the trees were close enough to cause a shadow. But I guess it could have been," Cam admitted.

Mrs. Peterson came over to the children. "What are you all going to do today?" she asked. "I'm going to head into the bush to work on my research. Hugh will stay here at the camp. He might do a bit of fishing at the sound later."

Talia looked at the other children. "I would really like to go have a look for the rushing water you mentioned, Mum," she said. "Would any of you like to come with me?"

"Yup, sure," said Cassia.

"Me, too," agreed Belinda. "Boys?"

Mish and Cam looked at each other. "To fish or not to fish?" said Cam.

"Thou must maketh a decision deep in thy valley," responded Mish.

The girls giggled and Rick humphed.

"I'd like to come with you girls," said Rick tentatively. "Even if Cam and Mish don't. Would that be okay?"

"I don't mind," answered Cassia, and the other two girls nodded.

"We might as well go with you," said Cam. "We can fish later, Mish. We're gonna be here for a while, so plenty of time!"

"Gotcha," said Mish.

Mrs. Peterson smiled at them. "Thy decision is made and lyeth in stone," she joked. "Please make sure you leave the campsite tidy before you go. Oh – and take one of the emergency locator beacons with you. I will have one with me as well while I sojourn into the bush."

She waved and went back to her big tent to gather what she needed for her morning's exploration.

The young people cleared away their breakfast things, making sure to leave the eating area clean and neat. A kea was back and attempted to fly off with a spoon just as Belinda went to pick it up. Luckily, the spoon was too heavy for the bird to carry and it dropped to the ground. The kea alighted on the ground beside the spoon.

"Do that again and I'll make you wash all the dishes," Belinda said to the cheeky bird. It looked at her and made a rude-sounding screech. Then it leaped into the air as Clumpy gave a short 'woof' right behind it. The kea flew down towards Clumpy, who turned and ran for his life, yelping. He disappeared into Cam's tent.

The children couldn't help laughing. Mr. Peterson emerged from the trees that went to the fjord just then, and asked, "What's the joke?"

Rick told him about the kea, the spoon and Clumpy. Mr. Peterson laughed. "Silly animals," he said. "So, where are you all off to? Anyone game to come fishing with me?"

Cam answered. "We are really looking forward to doing some fishing, Mr. Peterson. But we're going to do a bit of exploring first, to see if we can find the rapids Mrs. Peterson said she heard last night."

Mr. Peterson nodded. "All good. Got a locator

44

beacon?"

"Just going to grab one," said Talia. "Where are they, Dad?"

"Come with me," said her father, and the two of them walked to the area that had been designated for storage, covered by a big tarpaulin.

Meanwhile, the others put on suitable walking shoes and fetched jackets, just in case the weather turned cold, although it was pleasantly warm at that moment.

Cassia said, "Have you all got water bottles? We might need them."

"Good idea," said Belinda, and each of them grabbed a drinking bottle, filling it up with cold boiled water. Mrs. Peterson had boiled a few litres of stream water the previous evening and stored it in big bottles. She wasn't sure what germs might be floating downstream!

Finally, they were ready. Waving to her father, Talia called, "We're off, Dad! We'll be back in time for lunch, probably. Have fun fishing!"

He waved back and turned to trudge towards the fjord, carrying his fishing rod and a bag of bait.

"Can't wait to do that!" commented Cam. He loved fishing.

"You sure you don't want to go fishing now?" asked Mish.

Cam shook his head. "Nah, I'm keen to find some rapids," he replied. "Come on, Clumpy! You can come out now!"

An Odd Shadow

Clumpy's black head appeared at the door of the boys' dome tent, and he looked about cautiously. Was that annoying bird still around? But the kea had flown off, presumably to rejoin its friends. Clumpy ran over to the children joyfully and they all set off through the bush that Talia's mother had come out of the previous evening.

Chapter 7: The Waterhole

The six young people walked through the bushes that were near the camp, emerging into another open tussock area. Mish stopped. "Which way do we go?" he asked.

They all looked around, noting the winding ribbon that was their camp stream disappearing into the distance at their left, heading westwards through the tussock.

"Well, I don't think we are going to find rushing water in that stream any time soon," said Cassia. "So, maybe we should walk away from it, towards the mountains." She gestured to their right, where they could see hills and mountains rising in the east.

"Okay," said Talia. "Let's head towards that nearest slope, over there. Looks like some purple stuff on the ground. What's that? Plants of some kind?"

"I think they might be lupins," said Rick.

The Waterhole

Everyone turned and walked in the direction of the purple slope. It was about three football fields' lengths away. On either side of it there were other hills which then gave way to mountains that rose up into the sky majestically behind them. All of them were covered in trees and vegetation.

It was pleasant walking over the large flat tussock-covered area, which they could see now was in the lower part of a valley.

"Just think," said Rick. "All this stuff has been growing like this for thousands of years. Some of those trees look really tall! And some of this tussock looks pretty old as well."

"We are probably the first people to even look at these places close up," said Talia. As she had brought her camera with her, she stopped to take a photo. "Oh, hey, everyone!" she called to the others, who were still walking. "Listen! I think I can hear water!"

The other children paused. They could hear it, too. Everyone hastened to get to the purple hill.

When they reached it, they found that it was indeed covered by lupin plants. A few of the lupins had white flowers but most of them were purple.

"Pretty," said Cassia. She thought about picking some of the tall blooms then decided they looked prettier where they were.

Meanwhile, the three boys had gone around to the left of the slope, where the bush became denser at the foot of the adjacent hill, and the sound of water seemed louder. Mish gave a yell.

"Look at this!" he called loudly.

Belinda, Talia and Cassia hurried to catch up to the boys. As they came around the gentle curve of the lupin-covered hill, they realized it was really just a tall mound, sloping down to lower ground at its rear. The mound had been obstructing their view of a small river.

A short way along the river they could see a waterfall. The upper part of the river bubbled noisily over the top of a cliff about the height of a one-storey building, then fell straight down into a wide pool below, like a high-pressured shower. On the opposite side of the river, the pool was bounded by a hill with ancient-looking dense forest on its steep slopes, merging into what appeared to be a cliff right next to the waterfall. On the side where the young people were standing, there was a narrow grassy meadow covered by more purple and white lupins. Smaller rocks edged the meadow side of the river, while a few bigger rocks partially blocked the lower end of it, forming a natural dam. The water continued its downward flow between the outcropping rocks, then over a series of mossy boulders, producing a small stretch of white rapids, before eventually settling down sedately and disappearing into the trees a little further along.

"Oh, how gorgeous!" cried Belinda in delight.

"It sure is," said Talia.

"What a great swimming hole!" said Mish. "Should have

49

brought our togs with us." He took off his shoes and socks and put a foot into the water experimentally. "Hmm, cold but not too bad. I guess it's a bit sheltered by that little hill, so the sun warms it up a bit."

"And the water must sit around a bit before rushing down the stream," Cam added.

"What a great swimming hole!" said Mish. "Should have brought our togs with us."

Everyone took their footwear off and dabbled their feet in the pool, sitting on the small boulders that surrounded it, some of which were conveniently flat. Clumpy poked one paw into the water then leaped right in.

"Doesn't need his swimsuit," commented Mish. "Lucky

mutt!"

"Well, we could strip to our shorts and jump in, too," suggested Cam.

Rick noted how clear the water was. "I can see right to the bottom of this pool," he declared. "I wonder if there is gold in it? It looks a bit gravelly at the bottom."

Mish grinned at him. "Did you remember to bring your gold panning dish to camp?" he asked his younger brother.

"Sure did!" Rick grinned back. "The permit Dad asked for came last week. We're allowed to use my pan in this area just for this trip." He couldn't wait to get his pan and try his luck on the edge of the pool or even a little further downstream.

For a while the children just sat quietly on the rocks in the sunshine watching the waterfall.

The sound of the falling water reminded Cassia of a mild thunderstorm. She closed her eyes so that she could focus on it better. Then she opened them again. She had the oddest feeling she was being watched. She looked over towards the dark green trees on the far side of the pool but couldn't see anything past them.

"I feel like we're being watched," she told Belinda and Talia. "Do you see anything?"

Belinda looked around. The sun shone warmly on her back. All she could hear was the cheerful bubble of water. She felt very peaceful. "Not me," she said.

Cassia couldn't shake the feeling. "Talia? What about you? Do you sense anything?"

The Waterhole

Talia looked all around them carefully and shook her head.

"It's weird," said Cassia.

"Don't be so creepy, Cassia," said Belinda. "I bet there is no one else around for miles!"

"Sorry, Lindy," Cassia said sheepishly. "I'm not trying to be creepy."

Just then there was a whoosh above their heads as a beautiful bird with purple plumage on its back and a broad white breast flew past them. Its wings creaked as it flew. All three girls jumped, startled.

"It's a kereru; a wood pigeon," said Talia. "Maybe that's what you sensed watching us, Cassia."

Another kereru flew over their heads. They realized then that there were several of them around, perched on the high branches of the old trees opposite, eating berries.

"I guess," said Cassia. Her gaze strayed towards the waterfall. The cliff behind it appeared dark. She shook herself and determined to think of something else. "Reckon it would be fun to swim right under that waterfall," she said cheerfully.

Everyone else thought this was a great idea.

"How about we come back after lunch with our togs and have a real swim!" said Mish. "We should probably head back to camp now – by the time we get there it'll be morning teatime. I'm starving!"

"Me, too," agreed Rick.

Cam called out to Clumpy, who was paddling around in

circles in the middle of the pool. The dog looked back at Cam with his tongue hanging out happily and tried to woof. He paddled cheekily away from the children, getting quite close to the falling water. As they watched, he suddenly seemed to change his mind and came paddling back to them as fast as he could go. The black dog scrabbled out of the water quickly and ran to Cam, shaking water all over the fourteen-year-old as he reached him.

"Ugh!" complained Cam. "Couldn't you have shaken yourself before you got to me?"

Cassia and Belinda both noticed how the dog had suddenly turned back when he got near the waterfall. But neither of them said anything.

All of them put their shoes and socks back on and they began the short hike back to the camp. It was quite hot by now. They looked forward to going back to swim at the pool later.

When they arrived back at the campsite, it was to find the fold-up dining table already prepared with some packets of biscuits and a jug of juice. The boys immediately tucked in, but the girls returned to their tent where they brushed their hair and decided what clothes they were going to wear to the pool in the afternoon.

As it was only an hour or two till lunchtime, the children decided to stay near the campsite. Rick found his gold panning dish and tried to use it in the nearby stream. Mish saw him and urged him to take it closer to the sound, lest he muddy up their drinking water. Rick followed his advice.

Cam settled down on his mattress to read one of the books he had brought, but soon dozed off. It had been such an early morning for him! Mish came into the tent. He looked at the now sleeping Cam thoughtfully. Should he find a big spider and put it beside Cam's pillow? Or draw a moustache on his upper lip? He picked up the book Cam had been reading. It was one he had been hoping to read himself. Forgetting about playing a prank on Cam, he took the book over to his own bed and settled in for a good read.

An hour or so later, the girls came to the dome tent and put their heads in. "Wakey, wakey!" said Cassia loudly.

Cam woke with a start. He pulled himself up off his mattress with a big sigh before noticing Mish with his book. "Hey," he said. "That's *my* book."

Mish made his eyes like slits as he looked back. "Finders, keepers," he smirked. "You obviously found it boring – you fell asleep over it!"

Cam picked up his pillow to throw at his friend. Mish put the book down and grabbed his own pillow and the girls, who were still looking in at the entrance, began to cheer them on laughingly. Hearing the commotion, Clumpy ran into the tent as well. Just as he entered, a pillow flew across the tent and Clumpy jumped up and caught it in his teeth, causing the stuffing to fly everywhere. The girls roared with laughter.

"You owe me a new pillow!" growled Cam to Mish.

"Shoulda brought a spare," mocked Mish. "Now you're stuck with a leaking pillow for the trip. Captain Rod's not coming back just to bring you a pillow!"

Just then they heard a voice calling. Giving each other a friendly nudge, they followed the girls outside over to the eating area.

They found Mr. and Mrs. Peterson spreading the table with lunch food – bread, lettuce, tomatoes, and cheese as well as some rather scrumptious looking blueberry muffins.

"You been baking!" grinned Mish.

The two adults laughed. "It's amazing how resourceful one can be in the middle of nowhere," joked Mr. Peterson.

Cam noted the fishing rod leaning next to the tent and a covered chilly bin. "How did the fishing go, Mr. Peterson?" he asked.

"Got some red and blue cod!" boasted Mr. Peterson. "Good-sized specimens, too! Go and have a look."

The two older boys peeked into the large chilly bin. Sure enough, there were a few large fish lying in it. Both boys made up their minds to try their hand at fishing the following day.

"How did you get on today, Mum?" Talia asked her mother.

"Made a good start, pet," she answered. "There's more of certain sorts of plants here than I expected. They may have been around a lot longer than anyone thought. It's unlikely seeds somehow travelled to this remote area more recently!"

"Thanks for getting lunch ready for everyone," said Cassia. "May we start?"

"Of course!" replied Mr. Peterson. "Dig in."

They all tucked into lunch. As they ate, they told the adults all about the pool and waterfall.

"Sounds beautiful," said Mrs. Peterson. "I might go there for a swim, too, some time."

"We're going to go back after lunch," Talia told her mother. "It's in a sheltered area, so the sun should have warmed it even more by the time we get back to it!"

Rick remembered his gold panning. "I'm going to try panning there for some gold," he announced.

"That sounds like fun, too," commented Mr. Peterson. "I think I'll go have a nap!"

"Worn out already by your hard morning fishing?" teased his wife. "I'm going to write up some notes. Then I might join you for the nap."

"We'll clear up the lunch stuff," said Mish. "I think Cam and I are on dinner duty later, too. Aren't we, Cam?"

"Yep, sure are," said Cam. "May we use some of the cod, Mr. Peterson, please?" He already had an idea of what he wanted to cook.

"Absolutely," he answered. "That's what it's for. Thanks for putting the food away, kids." He got up from his chair and went inside the big tent.

The young people talked quietly as they busied themselves clearing away the meal. Then they went to their own tents and changed into swimsuits.

"Oh, no!" came Rick's muffled voice from his tent.

"What, little bro?" Mish asked, poking his head out of the blue dome tent.

"I forgot to bring a towel," said Rick shamefacedly. "Does anyone have a spare?"

"Yep, I do," answered Cam. "Well, actually, it was for Clumpy, but I'm sure he won't mind you using it." He pulled the towel out of his backpack and passed it to Rick.

Mish glanced at the towel. "Be careful you don't leave too much hair on that towel," he said. "Clumpy might only want dog hair on it."

Rick ignored his brother. "Thanks, Cam," he said. "And thanks, Clumpy," he added, bending down to pat the Labrador, who was lying contentedly in the shade.

Chapter 8: Feathery Matters

As soon as they were ready, the children, with Clumpy, returned to the pool. There were shouts of glee and laughter as they jumped into the cold water. Cam was the tallest of them and the pool was only a little higher than his head at its deepest point. But it was certainly a lot of fun to play and swim in. Each of them got right underneath the waterfall and trod water, allowing the falling jets to splash their heads and shoulders.

Clumpy was in his element, swimming from person to person, barking as they dunked each other amid much giggling. The kereru flew over them periodically.

"I think those birds' wings need oiling," commented Mish at one point. "They sound so creaky when they fly!" The others laughed and agreed with him.

They stayed there most of the afternoon, getting out of

the pool and lying on their towels in the sun for short periods before jumping back into the water.

Rick got tired of the pool before the others did. He put his glasses back on, having removed them for swimming, then walked a little further down the small river to try his hand at gold panning, having brought his pan with him. It wasn't long before he was engrossed in examining the contents at the bottom of it.

Belinda found a soft, grassy bed-like spot between two very tall lupin plants. She sighed as she plopped herself down on her towel and applied more sunscreen. Then she lay down on her stomach and stretched out. Closing her eyes, she listened to the sound of bird life in the nearby forest. Along with the regular creaking of the kereru wings, she could hear a multitude of chirps and tweets from what she figured must be smaller birds. While she had been in the pool, she had noticed a black-fronted robin or two hopping around on the ground on the forest side, looking for bugs. The bird melodies mingled with the harmonic tones of the rushing water. Belinda was nearly lulled into sleep when a shock of cold water hit her back.

"Hey!" she cried out, turning over to see who had splashed her. Four of the children were lying on their towels in other spots. She could see Rick downstream, still panning for gold. Even Clumpy was lying in the sunshine snoozing. She had no idea where the water had come from. Belinda sat up. Peering behind her in the other direction, she thought she perceived a movement in the lupins beyond.

"What's the matter, Lindy?" called Talia.

Belinda stood up. "Something put cold water on me," she complained. She walked further into the patch of tall lupins. There didn't seem to be anything there that was likely to have splashed her. But as she turned back towards the pool, she noticed a large feather on the ground. It was very pretty; purplish-blue in colour and seemed to have a sparkle.

But as she turned back towards the pool, she noticed a large feather on the ground.

"Look what I found," she said, going back to the others. "A very nice feather. Could it be from the kereru? Are they capable of dropping water on my back?"

Mish laughed. "More likely to drop something else on your back," he suggested.

"Ew," said Belinda in disgust. "Can someone please check my back?"

The Beak

Cassia got up to have a look. "Your back is fine," she said.

"Can I see that feather?" asked Rick, coming up to the group carrying his empty pan. He was intrigued by how sparkly the feather was. Belinda handed it to him.

Rick turned it around in his hand. "I wonder what kind of bird this came from," he said. "I don't think it was a kereru. It's not the same shade of purple."

"What do you think it is?" asked Belinda with interest.

Cam peered over Rick's shoulder at the feather. "It looks like it might have come from a pukeko, or a takahe," he suggested, referring to two species of native flightless birds. "We haven't seen any of those around here, though."

Rick was silent as he continued to turn the feather over in his hand.

"You can keep it if you want, Rick," said Belinda. "I'm not really into birds. But I would like to know what splashed water on my back!"

"Anyone want to swim again?" asked Mish. "Race you all to the waterfall and back!"

This appealed to everyone except Rick, who looked on with amusement as the others leaped back into the pool, including Clumpy, whose dog paddling was somewhat slower than the children's freestyle strokes. Clumpy was still paddling towards the waterfall when the young people had already reached it and were on their way back. They were all good swimmers.

"Haha, beat you, Clumpy!" taunted Talia as she passed the dog. Clumpy abandoned his attempt to reach the waterfall and turned around, following Talia back to the side of the pool. Talia leaned against a rock, panting, trying to catch her breath. The black dog paddled beside her, also panting. Talia giggled.

She splashed Clumpy and he sneezed. Scrambling out of the pool, the dog decided to do some exploring of his own. He trotted along the side of the pool towards the waterfall as Talia watched. To her surprise, just as he reached the side of the falls, he yelped as though startled then turned and ran back to her.

"What's the matter, Clumpy?" Talia asked the dog. "What did you see there?"

Cassia, who was floating on her back a short distance away, heard her. She swam over to Talia and Clumpy. "What's going on?" she asked.

"I was watching Clumpy walk towards the waterfall, and when he got there, he seemed to get scared by something and ran back," replied Talia.

Cassia laughed. "It was probably a butterfly or something equally harmless," she said. "Much as Cam hates to admit it, Clumpy really can be a wuss!"

Talia grinned at her. "It does seem that way," she agreed. "But we haven't had a look up that side of the waterfall. Wanna come with me and check it out?"

Cassia glanced towards the falling water. She could just make out the black rock behind it. Again, she had the odd feeling of being watched. She pushed the thought away.

"Sure," she said.

The two girls climbed out of the pool and gave themselves a quick rub with their towels. Barefooted, they walked gingerly along the edge of the pool, avoiding little sharp rocks, until they were within a metre or so of the falling water.

Talia looked down. "What's this?" she said. There were two more feathers on the ground in front of her, just like the one Belinda had found.

Cassia looked over her shoulder. "Okay, I guess that settles it," she said. "There must be some other kind of bird around here, hiding from us. Let's take the feathers back to your mum and see what she thinks of them."

By now everyone was out of the pool. Cam said, "Shall we go back now? Must be time for afternoon tea. I'm famished!"

"You're always hungry," commented Cassia.

"I'm famished, too," said Rick. He also looked a bit pink.

"Rick, did you put on sunscreen?" asked Cassia.

"Yep, kind of," said Rick. "When we first got here."

Mish rolled his eyes. "You're supposed to put it on every couple of hours. Didn't you see the rest of us putting more on?"

"Um, not really," admitted Rick. "Maybe that was when I was panning for gold."

"Did you find any gold?" asked Belinda, as she rubbed

her blonde hair with her towel.

"Not yet," said Rick. "But it was great fun trying!"

"I'd love to have a go at that, too," said Belinda. "Imagine if I could take a big gold nugget home to Mum!"

"Yeah, right," giggled Talia.

"Well, let's get going then," said Cam. "Rick, you might find that starts to sting a bit," referring to Rick's obvious state of sunburn.

"I'll be fine," averred Rick stoutly. He found his sandals and put them on. Then he picked up his T-shirt which he had thrown on the ground earlier and put it on, too. He winced a little as the material rubbed his pink shoulders.

Mish pretended he hadn't noticed, but Cassia said, "I think there is some aloe vera back at camp, Rick. That might help. Otherwise, you might find it really hard to sleep tonight!"

The rest of them gathered up their belongings and they all headed back to camp, feeling pleasantly tired.

When they got there, Mr. Peterson noticed Rick's pink face straight away. He whistled. "Looks like someone forgot to use the sunscreen! Didn't you put any on, Rick?"

"I did at first," said Rick. "But I didn't know you had to put more on after a while."

Cassia went into her tent and found her bottle of aloe vera. "Let me rub this on your shoulders, Rick," she offered.

He accepted gratefully and removed his T-shirt, somewhat painfully. He grimaced a little as Cassia gently

64

applied the aloe vera to his upper limbs, neck and back.

"Thanks, Cassia," he said to her.

"Hope it helps!" said Cassia. "Does anyone else need it?" No one did, so she gave the bottle to Rick in case he needed to put more on later.

There was a fresh jug of orange juice sitting on the camp table, along with some packets of potato chips. The children helped themselves.

Mrs. Peterson returned from her wanderings a short time later. She was wearing old jeans, a T-shirt, hiking boots and a big floppy hat. Her bare arms appeared somewhat sunburned, like Rick's.

"Uh-oh," said her husband. "Another person who could have used more sunscreen!"

"I forgot about it completely," she answered him. "But most of me was well-covered, so it's only my arms. They'll be okay." She was carrying a small box.

"What's in the box, Mum?" asked Talia.

"A few unusual leaves," Mrs. Peterson told her daughter. "Not very exciting for you, but quite exciting for me!"

"Um, okay," said Talia with a grin. "Would you like to know what we found?"

"What?" asked her mother with interest.

"Some very nice sparkly feathers," answered Talia. She pulled out the two she had found, and Rick brought out the one Belinda had given him as well. "Do you know what bird these might have come off, Mum? We thought at first they were from a kereru, but the purple is not the same."

Mrs. Peterson took the feathers and examined them. "The colours have similarities to takahe," she said. She held a feather up in the afternoon sunlight, noting how it sparkled.

"I wondered if they were from a takahe or a pukeko," said Cam.

"Maybe," said Talia's mother. "These seem to have quite a sparkle on them, though. They're rather large feathers, also. I wonder if there is another species of either of those around here? That would be an awesome find!"

"We'll keep an eye out, Mum," promised Talia.

Mrs. Peterson looked thoughtful as she regarded the sparkling feathers. "I think I will go on a special hunt to see if there are any takahe in this valley," she said.

"May we come, please?" asked Rick shyly. "I'd love to help discover a new species!"

"Of course," smiled Mrs. Peterson. "You can all come if you want to. But we may have to go quietly, lest we frighten any birds off."

"We might have to leave Clumpy behind then, Cam," Cassia said to her brother. "If he yelps or barks in fright it might scare any birds."

Cam sighed. "I guess," he agreed.

They discussed the bird hunt a bit longer then the three boys went to the chilly bins to collect the items they wanted to use for the evening meal.

After a pleasant evening, in which two kea came to see

if there were any tidbits available from the fried fish dinner, everyone decided to retire to their tents early. The atmosphere felt very relaxed. All the children except Rick fell asleep quickly. The swimming had worn them out! Rick, who was feeling the pain from the sunburn on his shoulders, turned over a few times with moans, but eventually found himself a comfortable position and fell asleep, too.

Chapter 9: The Shadow Returns

As usual, Cam was up early. He took Clumpy for a run beside the tussock stream, then returned to camp, heading for the portable toilet tent between the trees. A couple of minutes later, as he was about to turn around and leave the tent, he suddenly realized there was an oddly shaped shadow at the back of it. Something was behind the tent, and it didn't look like a tree! Again, part of it reminded him of a beak.

Cam shot out the front flap to race around the back of the tent. In his haste, he forgot about the tent ropes that were attached to pegs in the ground and tripped over one. Grunting in annoyance, he picked himself up. Behind the little tent, there was nothing unusual to be seen. Cam walked around the area cautiously but could not find anything that might have caused a shadow other than the nearby trees.

In his haste, he forgot about the tent ropes that were attached to pegs in the ground and tripped over one.

With a sigh, he returned to the main camping area.

Most of the others were up by now, either washing at the stream or looking for some breakfast. Cam went to the stream and had a wash, too.

Mrs. Peterson greeted Cam cheerfully. "How'd you sleep, Cam? I think you must be the earliest bird here!"

Cam grinned. "That's what Mum always says. I think I'm used to it 'cos I always take Clumpy for a walk in the mornings. I sleep okay, though."

"Who wants poached eggs for breakfast?" called Mr. Peterson's voice.

There was a chorus of "Me!" and "Yes, please!" as the rest of them came quickly to the eating area.

The children sat on the ground chatting as they ate breakfast.

Cam said casually, "I saw that shadow again this morning."

"Where?" asked Talia quickly. She looked around.

"I was in the loo tent," replied Cam. "The shadow was behind it, but I tripped over a rope trying to get around the back, and by the time I got there, there was nothing there."

Mish looked skeptical. "Are you having a joke on us, bro?"

"No," said Cam. "There is something around here."

Belinda glanced around also. "Well, what do you think it is?" she asked.

"I think it's some kind of big bird," said Cam. "It's tall."

Mish laughed. "A tall breed of takahe?"

Rick looked intrigued. "Well, those feathers were a similar colour to takahe, I think. But really sparkly."

"Maybe bird feathers get more sparkly when there are no humans around," suggested Mish innocently.

The others rolled their eyes. Just then, Mrs. Peterson came up to them. "How about you all do something around the camp area this morning, and after lunch we can go on a bird hunt?"

"We'd love to," said Cassia enthusiastically. "Cam was just telling us how he saw that mysterious shadow again. He thinks it's a tall bird."

Talia's mother sat down on a camp chair beside them. "What did you see, Cam?"

Cam explained. "Part of the shadow really looks like a beak. But it's quite high up on the shadow. So, it must be a tall bird."

"Maybe it's two birds – one standing on the shoulders of the other," ventured Mish.

Belinda and Talia giggled.

"Maybe it's just nothing," said Belinda. "Just a tree like we first thought."

"I think it's a moa," said Cam unexpectedly.

All the others looked at him in surprise and laughed loudly. "I knew you were pulling our leg, bro," said Mish. "Okay, well done, you had us wondering!"

Cam appeared to be examining the ground, fiddling with tufts of grass. Cassia looked at her brother. She recognized the obstinate expression on his face.

"You're really serious, aren't you, Cam?" she said to him. He nodded.

Mrs. Peterson glanced sideways at Cam. "Of course, you know moa have been extinct for hundreds of years? However, takahe were thought to be extinct as well, then they showed up again. I'd love to think moa might do the same." In her heart, though, she didn't think that was possible. Out loud, she said, "Well, we can have a good time looking, at least. So, what are you going to do this morning?"

Belinda turned to Rick. "Rick, I'd love to have a go at gold panning with you. Shall we go to that spot in the stream where you were yesterday?"

Rick looked pleased. "Yep!"

"Well, I'm all for some fishing," announced Mish. "Cam, you coming?"

"Sure," answered Cam, scrambling to his feet. He and Mish walked off together to get their fishing rods, joining Mr. Peterson as he appeared with his own gear. The three of them headed for the shore.

"Mum, Cassia and I can finish clearing up the breakfast stuff," Talia told her mother.

"Thanks, girls," said Mrs. Peterson gratefully. "In that case, I'll spend some time writing up notes." She disappeared into her tent.

Talia and Cassia chattered away happily as they washed the dishes and put away the breakfast things. Cassia rinsed the egg pot and walked over to a nearby bush to throw the water into it. She jumped backward in fright as the bush suddenly rustled and Clumpy emerged from it with a startled look on his face.

"What were you doing in there, Clumpy?" Cassia asked the dog. She soon found out what he was hiding from, as a kea swooped down, squawking loudly at Clumpy. The black dog quickly went under another bush.

"Ah, so the tables have turned," giggled Cassia.

72

"They're creeping up on *you* now." Turning to go back to Talia, she glanced over at the trees where the toilet tent was. There was an almost imperceptible movement just behind it. Cassia froze.

Talia looked over and saw Cassia standing quite still, staring at the toilet tent. "You okay, Cassia?" she called to her friend. Cassia still didn't move. Talia walked over to her.

"What are you looking at?" she asked, looking in the same direction as Cassia. Talia couldn't see anything except trees and the little tent.

"I saw a movement when I looked over there. Maybe Cam's right – maybe there is someone around. The movement was kind of high." Cassia's voice shook a little.

"Let's go have a look," suggested Talia. "With two of us, we should be okay."

Cassia hesitated. "I guess."

The two of them walked over to the tent. There was nothing behind it except more trees. No one seemed to be around, nor was there any bird sound.

"I don't see anything suspicious looking," remarked Talia.

Cassia looked back towards the main tent, in time to see a kea pick up a teaspoon. Forgetting her fright, she called out sharply to the bird. "Give that back, you!" Both girls raced towards the kea but it rose up into the air, still holding the teaspoon in its beak. Clumpy emerged from his bush to see what was going on. The kea swooped down

73

on him. It gave a raucous squawk and the teaspoon fell to the ground. Talia ran and snatched it up quickly. She smirked at the kea. It flew to a nearby tree and glared back at her.

"Thanks, Clumpy!" she said to the black dog, ruffling his head and patting him. Clumpy wagged his tail, pleased at the praise, although he didn't know what he had done to earn it. He checked to see what the kea was doing, but it had flown off.

"Score to us!" giggled Cassia. "What would you like to do now, Talia?"

Talia considered. "How about we go check out how the others are all getting on?"

"Okay," agreed Cassia. "Come on, Clumpy!"

The two girls strolled leisurely towards the stream, where Belinda and Rick were happily taking turns panning.

"Got anything, Lindy?" asked Cassia.

"Not yet," answered Belinda. "But it's great fun trying! I can see why people in the old days got so caught up in it. Always hoping for that shiny speck to show up in the bottom of the pan!"

Rick, who was shaking out the pan just then, gave an exclamation. "Maybe this time!" he said excitedly.

The girls crowded around him as he jostled out the remainder of the pan contents. Sure enough, there was a tiny but clearly visible speck of gold in the pan. Clumpy put his nose forward and tried to sniff it.

"Get away, Clumpy!" Rick pushed the dog away. "Don't

74

want to lose my very first bit of gold!"

Talia giggled. "And possibly your only piece of gold," she commented. "Can Cassia and I have a turn?"

"Please?" grinned Cassia.

"Wait a sec," said Rick. He produced a little jar that he had brought, filling it with water. He carefully pressed his finger onto the gold speck in the pan, then dipped his finger into the water in the jar. The speck came off his finger and quickly sank to the bottom.

"Ooh," said Talia. "Is it okay if I try now? Can you show me how to do it, please, Rick?"

Rick showed her how to gather some of the gravel and stone mixture from the stream bed and jostle it back and forth with the water, gradually emptying the pan. "Because gold is heavy, the shaking causes it to go to the bottom," he explained, passing the pan to Cassia.

Cassia had a turn. "It's kinda fun, but I think I'll leave you to enjoy it," she remarked.

"Me, too," agreed Talia. "Cassia, let's head down to the fjord and see how the fishermen are doing!"

They left Belinda and Rick to pan to their hearts' content, while they continued walking along the little stream until they reached the shore. Clumpy followed them, quickly running up to Cam as he caught sight of the boy sitting on a rock with his fishing rod.

"Hey, Clumpy!" Cam greeted his pet. "Come to help us fish?"

"Looks like Mish doesn't need any help," commented

Talia, as she observed Mish lying back with his eyes closed, his fishing rod wedged firmly between some smaller rocks.

Mr. Peterson was a little further along. His line was jiggling. Talia went over to him. "Have you caught a fish, Dad?"

Her father reeled in the line. His fishing rod bent into a curve under the weight of whatever he had caught. The line jumped around as the creature tried to escape. It did not escape, however, and soon Mr. Peterson was holding up a large trevally for the children to see.

Mish opened his eyes briefly, eyed the fish, checked his own rod, then closed his eyes again. "Some people have all the fun," he muttered.

"Yippee!" shouted Cam, as his line began jerking. Mish sat up straight. He gave Cam's rod an exaggerated glare as the boy reeled in his catch.

"What's that one, Cam?" asked Cassia.

"It's a red moki," said Mr. Peterson, coming up behind her. "Well done, Cam!"

Mish looked at his line, which was not moving in the slightest. "Maybe I need a new fishing rod," he commented.

The others laughed. "I'm sure you'll catch something eventually," said Mr. Peterson.

Talia and Cassia watched Cam reset his line. Then they went over to the big flat rock where the fishing boat had dropped them all off. Sitting down on the edge of it, they dangled their legs into the sea water. On the other side of the fjord, they could see seals frolicking around in the water.

"How gorgeous!" said Cassia. The two girls stayed there for quite a while, enjoying the relaxed atmosphere and the seals' antics.

"How gorgeous!" said Cassia. The two girls stayed there for quite a while, enjoying the relaxed atmosphere and the seals' antics. Meanwhile, Mr. Peterson continued to reel in fish after fish at regular intervals.

"Looks like you're having a great fishing expedition!" called Talia to her father.

"I certainly am!" he responded. "No shortage of fish for breakfast, lunch and dinner! But right now, I'm ready for a cuppa. Anyone want to come back to camp with me for morning tea? We can leave our lines sitting in the water, boys. Maybe something will be on them when we come back!"

Mish sighed. His line began jerking at that very moment, and he quickly began to reel it in. "A blue cod!" He exclaimed in relief. "Now I'll happily go have morning tea!" The others laughed.

He and Mr. Peterson reset their fishing lines, then the little crowd made its way eagerly back up the stream to the campsite, calling Belinda and Rick on the way.

"Oh, my goodness!" exclaimed Cassia crossly, running to the food area. A bag of peanuts was ripped apart on the ground, with peanuts strewn everywhere. Three kea were happily eating them.

"Go buy your own peanuts!" Cassia scolded the birds. She flapped her arms and the kea flew off.

Mrs. Peterson came out of her tent. "What's going on?"

"Just those naughty kea, Mum," Talia told her. "Stealing our peanuts now!"

"Oh, dear," said her mother. "I was looking forward to those, too. Are there any peanuts left?"

Talia rummaged around in one of the food containers. "Yes, there are some more packets here," she said. "But I think we'll have to be careful to make sure we put lids back on containers properly, else they will be right into everything!"

"Good idea," said her mother. "Well, everyone, on another note – I'm done researching plants and writing notes for the moment. How would you all like to begin our bird hunt now, instead of after lunch? We could take a few things with us to eat."

"Well – we just came back for some morning tea," said her husband. "How about we have a good feed now, so you don't have to take too much with you?"

The children approved of this plan and in a short time they were all eating sandwiches.

"We can take an apple each for later," suggested Talia.

After their very early lunch, everyone except Mr. Peterson put on clothes suitable for hiking, plus sturdy footwear. Just before they left, they all went down to the shore to check the fishing lines.

Mish ran forward eagerly when he noticed his line moving. "*Now* they decide to start biting!" he exclaimed. Reeling it in, he was elated to see another red moki, even bigger than Cam's.

"Good going," laughed Cam. "Mr. Peterson, do you want us to pull our lines in, or leave them here with you?"

"I can bring them in for you," he answered generously. "Or Clumpy can, since he's staying with me. Now – Valerie, do you have locator beacons?"

"Yes, dear," his wife answered. She gave her husband a quick kiss. "Have fun fishing! Wish us well in our moa hunt!"

"I think you'd need a miracle to find one of those," he laughed. Waving at them and calling Clumpy over to him, he turned to settle back down on the comfortable spot he had found, making room for the dog to lie down beside him. The last view Cam had of Clumpy was of the black dog stretched out with his eyes already closed.

Chapter 10: Bird Hunt

Once back at the campsite, Mrs. Peterson paused at the folding table to spread out a map of the area. The map showed the contours of the land – where it was low, high or flat.

"Look at this, kids," she said to them. "You can see your waterfall river over here. It appears to have a very tall hill on the other side of it. There appears to be another valley beyond that hill, just to the right of it, jutting up against something high just on the other side of the waterfall river."

"There are lots and lots of tall dark trees on the other side of the river, going up the side of a really steep hill," commented Talia. "They go right along almost to the side of the waterfall, where it looks like it turns into cliff. You'd have to do some hard climbing to try and get over it all!"

Bird Hunt

Rick peered at the map closely. "I see what you mean about a valley on the other side of the steep hill and cliff, Mrs. Peterson," he agreed. "But it looks like on the map, on this side of the river where we were swimming, the meadow goes along for a bit kinda flat then opens out into another bigger, wider area."

Mrs. Peterson nodded. "I think, if we are going to find any flightless birds, they're likely to be on this side, in that wide valley. While birds that can't fly might be able to climb steep hills and cliff faces, it seems likely to me they'd find an easier way to go!"

This made sense to everyone. They finished getting ready to embark on the hunt. Each person made sure their water bottle was full, sunhats or caps were on, an apple and muesli bar were in each of their pockets, locator beacons were being carried by Mrs. Peterson and Cam as planned, then they all headed off energetically in the direction of the waterfall. Rick had put on a copious amount of sunscreen!

They made their way across the tussock field towards the purple mound that hid the river from sight. As they rounded the small rise, the vista of colourful lupins backed by the pool with its waterfall and short stretch of rapids came into view, evoking a gasp of admiration from Mrs. Peterson.

"What a beautiful spot, kids!" she cried. "No wonder you wanted to come swimming here. Now I do, too."

Talia laughed at her mother. "How about you drag Dad

away from the fishing later and bring him here for a romantic swim?"

"I might just do that," grinned her mother. She paused for a few moments to admire the view, noting the steep forest-covered hill opposite. "I see what you mean about cliff on the other side, near the waterfall. Flying birds could reach the other side obviously, but I doubt if a flightless bird like a takahe could climb it." She then gestured towards the narrow meadow of lupins that stretched away to their right. "Let's keep going that way for now."

Following her lead, the young people turned to the right and pushed their way through the plentiful lupins. They seemed to go on for some time before the meadow opened out again into a wider valley. Here there was more tussock, along with the odd patch of grassy gravel, from which sprouted more lupins.

"So pretty," commented Belinda, as she stopped to take some photos with her cell phone. She had been conserving the phone's battery power by keeping it turned off most of the time, as had the others who had brought cell phones with them.

"No sign of any more feathers, though," added Cassia. She had been looking at the ground carefully as they walked.

"There's the river again," spoke up Rick. The others followed his gaze, to where the river snaked out from some trees a short distance away, then curved around before disappearing into tussock.

"I wonder if we should keep alongside that river," said Mrs. Peterson. "It would be easier to find our way back."

"Sure thing," said Mish. He turned towards the river.

Cam followed him, glancing around. The land appeared deserted. He could see the movement of flying birds in the trees, and hear little high-pitched chirps, but there didn't seem to be any other animal life around. He wondered whether he had imagined the whole shadow thing after all! Maybe the feathers did belong to a creaky wood pigeon.

They all trudged on, following the path of the river. Sometimes it curved right into the forest for a short distance, where the little group gazed up in awe at tall, ancient-looking trees, but it always emerged again into the tussock valley at some point.

After they had walked for well over an hour, Talia came to a stop. They had just reached an area of the valley where the tussock ended, and what appeared to be grassy swamp lay ahead of them.

"Mum, can we stop for a rest please? I feel like we've been walking for hours." She could see agreement in the other children's faces.

Her mother paused and glanced around at them all. She was used to hiking and had been engrossed in the untouched flora around her. "Of course, pet," she said cheerfully.

With a sigh of relief, the children sank down onto the grass.

Rick pulled out his muesli bar. As he munched

contentedly, he stared out over the swamp. Then he gave a start. "What's that over there?"

Everyone looked at him and said, "Where?" in unison.

Cam looked out over the swamp and saw what Rick was seeing. "Some kind of dark-blue bird!" he said excitedly.

Mrs. Peterson pulled out her binoculars. "Maybe pukeko?" She trained the binoculars on the blue patches. "Hmm, no, too plump for pukeko."

"Let's try to get closer," suggested Mish.

They all began entering the swampy area towards the blue creatures, trying to keep low.

"Ugh," muttered Belinda. "This is quite wet!"

Talia's mother glanced over at her sympathetically. "Welcome to the world of research and discovery, Lindy!" she smiled.

"I don't think it's any worse than when we first looked for what was causing the glint," commented Talia.

"That's true, I suppose," agreed Belinda.

They pushed their way through rushes and long grasses, gradually nearing the blue birds. Finally, Mrs. Peterson motioned them to stop. She had another look through the binoculars, then exclaimed to herself quietly.

"What is it, Mum?" Talia asked her. "What are they?"

"I'm pretty sure they're takahe, but they're a long way from where they usually are. I think this is a completely different group, most likely undiscovered before now. There are no tags on their legs!" Mrs. Peterson looked utterly delighted. "Here, each of you have a look." She passed the binoculars to Rick, who had a look and passed them on.

"Can we take photos?" asked Cassia.

"I think we'll have to get closer yet," said Mish. He already had his cell phone out, set to record video.

"Well, try and stay as quiet as possible, and move slowly," cautioned Mrs. Peterson.

This they did, but the dark-blue plump birds didn't seem bothered by them at all, even when Rick slipped and grabbed onto a bunch of grass to steady himself. They were very close now – only a few metres away.

Cam looked out over the swamp and saw what Rick was seeing.
"Some kind of dark-blue bird!" he said excitedly.

Mish found a dry patch of ground to sit on and began to video record the birds. He zoomed in on their legs, noting the lack of tag, which government conservation officers usually put on these kinds of birds.

The Beak

Meanwhile, Cam had been taking a close look at the colours of the birds' feathers. While they certainly had dark-blue plumage, he couldn't see any evidence of sparkle, and he was sure they weren't purple like the feathers they had found. There was also a good deal of variegated green feather on their backs. He thought it was wonderful that they may have discovered a new flock of takahe, but they looked very much like the ones he had seen in his local wildlife park.

They stayed with the takahe for quite a while, watching the peaceful creatures as they poked amongst grass and other plants. Mrs. Peterson was quietly taking notes. Presently, she said, "Okay, let's make a count. How many can you see? Adults and juveniles?"

The children counted carefully. "I see five smaller ones, and fourteen big ones," said Belinda.

"Me, too," agreed Cassia. "Oops, no – look, another big one just appeared from behind that clump of reeds, with two little ones. Those are smaller than the other juveniles. How cute!"

Mish looked towards where she was pointing and aimed his phone at the two very small takahe. The younger birds were pretty much one colour all over – a very dark blue, almost black. Their beaks were a greyish hue rather than the bright scarlet of the adult birds.

"How fluffy the young ones are!" said Talia.

"That's to keep them warm," said Mrs. Peterson. "I'm sure it gets very cold in this area at times!"

Belinda remarked, "Sitting here looking at them all, I can see that each of the adults is just a little different. Like, some have really red beaks, but others have some light brown. And their back feathers aren't all identical to each other either."

Rick agreed with her. "At home, Dad keeps java sparrows. Most of the time I can't tell one from another."

Mish laughed. "Just as well he doesn't keep takahe. Mum would probably name them all!"

"Well, this has been a wonderful find," said Mrs. Peterson. "But I think we'd better be heading back. Not sure of the weather either – look at the sky." They looked.

"Uh-oh. We might be in for a wetting," said Talia.

They gathered up their things that they had laid on the ground and began their journey back to the camp. Within a very short time, raindrops began to fall, increasing in size and frequency until they merged to become a proper rain shower. Mish tucked his cell phone under his shirt. He didn't want to lose his video clips of the takahe! The others also checked to make sure their devices were not getting wet. Everyone pulled their jacket hoods over their heads as the shower turned into a decidedly heavy downpour.

Chapter 11: Rainstorm

It wasn't a very pleasant hike back. And when they finally reached the waterfall area, they stopped in shock. The small river had become a raging torrent, pouring over the top of the cliff not only into the pool, but onto the narrow lupin meadow. The pool itself had risen until the water had breached its usual boundary of rocks. Already the adjacent lupin meadow was covered in water.

"This doesn't look good," commented Mish. "Are we going to try wading through that?"

"I'd prefer we didn't," answered Mrs. Peterson. "But I can't see any other way. We'll go a little way into the lupins but then I think we'll have to climb over the mound instead of going around it. Stay together everyone!"

They splashed through the ankle-deep water surrounding the lupins in the narrow meadow. Meanwhile, the rain increased in intensity.

"I really hope our phones and cameras don't get too wet!" said Belinda mournfully. She had just reached the mound when she slipped. "Ohh!"

Mish, who was in front of her, turned. He grabbed her by the arm quickly and pulled her to her feet.

"Thanks, Mish," said Belinda gratefully. "Now I'm really sopping!"

They were all soaked through by the time they reached the campsite. Here they found Mr. Peterson and Clumpy sitting inside the food awning area out of the rain. They greeted the travellers cheerfully.

"Got a drenching, I see," grinned Mr. Peterson. "Better get out of those wet clothes pronto, kids. Don't want you catching pneumonia! I'll boil up the kettle for some hot drinks."

The children made haste to their own tents where they hurriedly changed into dry clothes. Outside, the rain came down in a heavy torrent.

Belinda, now warm and comfortable in dry clothes, peeked out her tent door. "I'm not sure I want to leave this tent even to get a hot drink or dinner!" she said to the other two girls. "Shall we wait a bit?"

Cassia and Talia nodded in agreement. "I'm really tired anyway, after that big hike," said Talia. "Happy to lie right here on my warm sleeping bag for a while!"

Belinda poked her head out of the tent again. She called to the others. "We're gonna wait a while! Too wet to come

90

out." She could see Rick, well bundled up in his jacket, sitting under the awning drinking what must be hot chocolate and munching a chocolate biscuit. "Hmm, tempting," thought Belinda. She turned back to her friends. They were both lying on their beds with their eyes closed. Belinda decided to do the same.

Over at the food area, Rick was telling Mr. Peterson about the takahe. Mish checked his cell phone. It appeared to be in good order.

"I took some video footage, Mr. Peterson," Mish said to him. "Have a look."

The little group peered at the small screen. "That's remarkable!" commented Mr. Peterson. "Lucky you! Valerie, I bet that made your day," he said aside to his wife.

She smiled. "It really did. No tags, so I'm pretty sure this lot hasn't been seen before. It'll be a shame to have to let someone know they're here, but best to get them officially recorded as well."

"Aw, does that mean other people will start coming here a lot?" asked Rick.

"Not necessarily," replied Mrs. Peterson. "Only a few conservation bird specialists, most likely. The birds might get a mention on the News, though."

Mr. Peterson turned to Cam. "So, Cam! Did you find the owner of the mysterious feathers?"

Cam was quiet for a moment. Then he said, "I really don't think so. The colours are just different. And it doesn't explain the shadow. The takahe birds aren't tall.

And they were a long way away from here. I don't see how one of them could have sprinted there and back so fast!"

"Maybe there's a rogue one, that's in disgrace from the rest of his family?" suggested Mish. "'Cos it's taller than the rest? Like a takahe mutation!"

"Yeah, right," said Rick. "Anyway, our dad will be really thrilled to see Mish's video."

"I'm sure he will," smiled Mrs. Peterson. "Wow, it's really quite wet now, isn't it? I don't blame the girls for wanting to stay in their tent!"

"Speaking of tents, are your tents watertight, boys?" asked her husband.

"Yeah, I think so," said Cam. "The ground is firm and a little higher just over there."

Mrs. Peterson glanced towards the stream nearby. "What about our cold food store? Any chance of the chilly bins getting washed away?"

"I'll be really brave and go check," answered her husband. He popped into the big tent adjoining the awning and emerged wearing a sturdy raincoat. Pulling its hat over his head, he headed for the stream. He returned a few minutes later, to report that while the stream was a little faster than usual, the chilly bins were still firmly in place.

"What are we going to do now?" asked Rick. "I don't want to sit in my tent by myself while it rains."

"We brought the cards," answered Mish. "Can we all play cards in one of the big tents?"

92

Mrs. Peterson thought for a moment of her notes. She had an urge to write some more. Then she checked herself. "Of course, we can all play cards," she said with a smile. "Our tent is big. Do you want to see if the girls want to join us?"

Cam regarded the falling rain. It seemed to be slowing. He made a run for the girls' tent, calling to them to let him in. Cassia quickly opened the zip. The three girls had all been resting but were awake.

"Want to come and play cards with the rest of us?" said Cam. "In Talia's parents' tent. We're just gonna start."

They all did. Putting on their still damp jackets, they dashed over to the Petersons' tent. Meanwhile, Mish had fetched the cards from the tent he shared with Cam, and now everyone, including Clumpy, spread themselves around on the floor. Clumpy settled himself between Mish and Cam and went to sleep.

"What shall we play first?" asked Rick.

There was a bit of discussion about games, before settling on one to play. All of them became quite engrossed, so no one noticed that the rain had slowed down to a steady drizzle as the day faded.

Finally, after being soundly beaten for the fourth time, Belinda said, "I have to use the bathroom. Ugh, that's the only bad thing about camping – running through the rain to get to places!" She peeked outside. "Oh – the rain has nearly stopped. Be right back!" She decided the rain wasn't heavy enough to need a jacket and made a dash across the grass to the toilet tent. Once inside, the late afternoon sun broke through momentarily, lighting up the side of the tent in a weird way. Belinda glanced up, thinking how pretty it was, then it was her turn to freeze, as Cassia had done. There was a shadow outside – nearly as tall as the tent! As she watched, it moved. Belinda waited for the sound of the ground crunching but heard nothing. Then the shadow moved away and she could no longer see it. Trembling, Belinda sat for a few minutes. The shadow didn't come back. She breathed deeply a few times, telling herself there was nothing to be scared of.

When she emerged from the tent, she peered bravely around the side. There was nothing there that she could see. Belinda didn't have the slightest intention of searching by herself in the darkening trees. After another brief look, she ran back to the others.

"Okay, Cam and Cassia, I believe you," she said breathlessly, and a little shakily. "When I was in the loo, there was a moving shadow outside. It went away. I couldn't tell what it was, but it was tall."

Mr. and Mrs. Peterson looked at each other. Each knew what the other was thinking – they didn't want the children in danger from some unknown intruder.

Mish was lazing back against a big cushion, glaring at his hand of cards with disapproval. "Not likely to win with this hand," he thought. Out loud, he remarked, "Don't worry, Lindy. It's probably just Cam's moa coming to see what's for dinner."

94

The Beak

Cam threw his own cushion at Mish. "You might have to eat your words," he retorted.

Mrs. Peterson grasped onto the humour. "Well, we'd better get onto our dinner before the moa does then," she grinned. "Hugh, while the kids and I fish around – literally – for some fish for dinner, would you like to take a look in the trees?" She looked at her husband meaningfully.

Belinda didn't have the slightest intention of searching by herself in the darkening trees.

He nodded. "I'll use the bathroom myself while I'm at it," he said. He disappeared outside.

Mrs. Peterson glanced at the girls. Talia seemed unconcerned, but she recognized the other girls' fear, although they were trying to put on a brave face. "How about you girls come and help me get dinner ready? Boys,

95

can you light the lanterns under the awning, please?"

Nodding, the boys each turned on one of the hanging lamps outside under the awning. The lights swayed merrily, casting cheer on the dull evening. Little insects flew quickly towards the light, in addition to a few large moths.

"That's a very large moth!" said Rick, looking at a moth with green and yellow wings. "What kind is it?"

Mrs. Peterson and the girls emerged from the tent to have a look. "Hmm, never seen one like it before!" said Mrs. Peterson. "Maybe a new moth species! Come on, girls, let's grab the food."

Talia, Belinda and Cassia followed her, and soon their minds were focused on preparing a meal. Talia chattered to her two friends about cooking, and soon they had all nearly forgotten about the shadow.

They remembered briefly when Mr. Peterson finally reappeared. He looked relaxed and not worried at all.

"I had a pretty thorough look around over there," he announced to everyone. "Nothing at all out of the ordinary, not even a footprint. Not sure what you saw, Belinda – maybe a trick of the light? I can't see anything we need to be concerned about anyway. Besides, wouldn't Clumpy alert us somehow? That's what he's here for, after all."

Belinda sighed in relief. "I'm so glad," she said. "Actually, the sun was shining weirdly on the side of the tent. It was that that made me look up in the first place.

Maybe it was just an optical illusion, after all." She felt better as soon as she said it.

Cassia felt relieved also. She glanced over at her brother. Cam didn't say anything. He was patting Clumpy.

Mr. Peterson looked at the delicious-looking meal of fish and potato salad on the folding table. "That looks really good, girls! Can we eat now?"

There was a chorus of assent, and the folding chairs were pulled out. Everyone became more relaxed as they talked and laughed while enjoying the meal. The rain began to fall again as they ate.

At one point, Cassia looked over towards the small toilet tent. Mr. Peterson had turned on the lantern hanging inside it, and the light did cast some odd-looking shadows. She could see insects flying around outside, too, trying to get into the tent to get to the light. Beyond the tent was darkness. Cassia didn't see any movement at all.

When it was time for everyone to turn in for the night, Mrs. Peterson asked casually, "Do you kids all think you'll be okay to sleep in your tents tonight? Or do you need to share ours?"

Talia looked indignant. "We'll be okay, Mum!"

Mish and Cam laughed. "We'll be okay, too," said Mish. "Big Brave Clumpy will save us. Actually, maybe Clumpy should sleep with Rick? Or the girls?"

"I suspect Clumpy will sleep exactly where he wants to sleep," said Cam. "Okay, boy, whose tent is it to be tonight?"

Clumpy looked at Cam and wagged his tail. Then he headed straight over to the girls' tent, stopping at the door which had been zipped up to keep out the rain.

"Humph!" said Cam.

Cassia giggled. "Guess it's our turn tonight. Thanks, Clumpy! Knew we could count on you!"

Because of the drizzling rain, no one wanted to spend time washing at the stream. It wasn't long before all the tents were occupied, each showing a faint light as their occupants got ready for bed.

In the girls' tent, Belinda was ruffling Clumpy's ears. "I am surprised Clumpy chose our tent, Cassia," she said. "What made him do that?"

Cassia reached over to stroke the black Labrador. He licked her face. "Clumpy has always known when I was upset or nervous," she said. "I guess he just wanted to look after us." She snuggled down into her sleeping bag. "Goodnight, Talia, Lindy and Clumpy!" Returning her goodnights, the other girls also snuggled down and it wasn't long before all of them were asleep.

Mr. Peterson went for a final walk around the campsite before turning off the lanterns. He stood still under the awning for a few moments, listening. Hearing nothing but the drip-drip of rain, he, too, turned in for the night.

Chapter 12: After the Drizzle

The rain continued for the next few days. The children were glad they had brought warm clothes and jackets. It was true that even at the beginning of summer, this part of the country could get very cold! The girls spent most of their time inside the tents, playing cards, or one of the few board games they had brought, or reading books. Rick was quite happy to stay with them. Mrs. Peterson didn't seem to notice the weather and was out every day from early in the morning doing her research, usually appearing at mealtimes sodden and dripping, but still cheerful.

Although Mish and Cam didn't mind reading books, they both preferred to be outside.

"I feel like we're losing all this good camping time staying inside," Mish grumbled to Cam on the second day of heavy rain. He had just lost yet another game of cards to Talia.

Mr. Peterson heard him. "I'm with you on that one, Mish," he agreed. "But you know what, a keen fisherman doesn't let a little rain stop him!"

"Or her, Dad," Talia put in, from her perch on a soft cushion. "I like fishing, too!"

"So, who's up for some fishing, rain or no rain?" asked Mr. Peterson with a grin.

"Uh – I think I'll stay here," said Talia sheepishly.

"I'm definitely up for it!" said Mish.

"Count me in," said Cam.

"Anyone else?" Mr. Peterson looked around. "Clumpy?"

Belinda giggled. Clumpy looked supremely happy, stretched out on a warm blanket, fast asleep. She doubted if he would want to go out into the rain! "I'll stay here, too," Belinda said.

"I wouldn't mind fishing some time while we're here," said Talia. "Just not today. Cassia, how about you? Want to go sit with your brother in the cold?"

"Probably no more than Rick wants to sit with *his* brother in the cold," smiled Cassia. "Is that right, Rick? Rick?" Rick was so engrossed in his book that he hadn't heard her at all. "Rick?" Cassia said a little more loudly.

Rick looked up vaguely. "What?"

"The other guys are going fishing. Do you want to go?" Cassia asked patiently.

"No, thanks," Rick said and returned to his reading.

The Beak

"Just us again then, boys," said Mr. Peterson to Mish and Cam. The three of them donned their jackets and trooped out into the rain. It was not as heavy now, but still quite persistent. However, once they arrived at the edge of the sound with their fishing rods, the rain no longer mattered to them. There were trees overhanging some of the rocks, providing a bit of shelter, so it wasn't long before all three had found a good spot to sit and had their lines out. Cam pulled his woolly hat down over his ears and the hood of his rain jacket over that. It was still a bit chilly!

Mish looked out over the water. There was something soothing about watching rain droplets fall onto the calm sea, causing millions of tiny ripples that spread out and bumped each other. Apart from the rain, it was very quiet. Even the birds seemed hushed up by the weather. He breathed a sigh of contentment. This was much better than being cooped up in a tent!

Mish, Cam and Mr. Peterson did a lot of fishing in spite of the rain. But by the fourth day of drizzle, everyone except Mrs. Peterson was becoming restless and a bit grumpy.

"Clumpy, you've put your wet paws on my pillow *again*," Mish scolded the dog when he got into his sleeping bag one night. "Why can't you just sit on Cam's pillow? It was leaking anyway! We might have to get your towel off Rick. It's not like he's swimming with it!"

"Rick still needs the towel to wash and dry himself,"

101

responded Cam. He added hopefully, "Would you like my pillow instead? It's dry."

"Oh, hahaha," retorted Mish. "And give *me* the pillow with hardly any fluff left in it? Nope!"

Finally, the rain ceased. Belinda woke to feel the warmth of the morning sunshine on her arm, which was leaning against the side of the tent. She poked her head out the door. The sun was streaming down on the campsite. It was going to be a beautiful day!

She saw a kea pecking around the food area. "I bet you've missed our food," she thought. They had been having their meals inside the big tent during the rainy days. Belinda thought about the mysterious shadow. No one had said anything about it; it seemed to have been forgotten, even by Cam.

She heard a movement behind her and turned to see Cassia yawning and stretching her arms out. "Is it still raining?" she asked Belinda.

"Nope, finally stopped!" said Belinda.

Talia pulled herself out of her sleeping bag. "About time," she said cheerfully. "Ooh, what's that?" as a shadow darkened one side of the tent. The other girls looked up alertly.

"Wakey, wakey!" came Mish's voice. "It's going to be an awesome day! Get up!"

Cassia put her arms back inside her sleeping bag. "What's the hurry," she murmured. Her sleeping bag felt so warm and comfortable.

The Beak

"Can I come in?" asked Cam from just outside the door.

Belinda unzipped the tent door for him. Mish and Rick were with him. Rick looked excited.

"What's going on?" asked Belinda, puzzled.

"Talia, your mum saw the shadow when she was in the loo tent this morning!" Rick blurted out. "She thinks something is definitely around here and wants us to all have a really good look together."

Cassia's head jerked upwards. "Oh, no, really? What does she think it is?" Her face looked scared.

"It's okay, Cassia," said her brother reassuringly. "She thinks it's some type of stealthy animal. But since it hasn't tried to hurt any of us or get our food, she doesn't think it's dangerous. And it doesn't seem to like rain, 'cos we haven't seen it around."

"Well, we haven't been outside to see if it was in the rain," observed Belinda. "We've all been inside most of the time, or you guys were down at the sound. Maybe it doesn't like water?" Her brow furrowed.

"Anyway, get up and come have breakfast," said Mish impatiently. "Then we can see what Mrs. Peterson wants to do. It will give us something different to do, anyway!"

It wasn't long before everyone was once again sitting around the fold-up table under the big awning, eating eggs fried with fish.

"I never thought I'd say this, but I don't think I want to eat fish again for quite a while after this trip," sighed Mrs. Peterson. "I'm all fished out!"

103

After the Drizzle

"We're out of cereal, dear," grinned her husband. "So there may be a few fishy days yet. Someone ate all the cereal!"

"Probably the kea," suggested Mish. "I'm sure none of us would do a thing like that."

Mrs. Peterson rolled her eyes. "Of *course* none of you would," she said drily. "Maybe it was Clumpy. Maybe Clumpy even fed it to the kea."

"Where *is* Clumpy?" asked Cassia, looking around for the black dog. "Oh, there he is. And look what that kea is up to, haha!"

The kea tried to peck Clumpy's nose, but the dog was wiser now, ducking out of reach and running underneath Cam's chair.

The Beak

Everyone chuckled as they watched Clumpy wolfing down a piece of fish someone had dropped on the ground. A kea hovered just above him, its beady eye also on the fish. There was an angry caw as the fish disappeared down Clumpy's throat. The kea tried to peck Clumpy's nose, but the dog was wiser now, ducking out of reach and running underneath Cam's chair.

"Silly dog," said Cam affectionately, patting his pet's furry black head.

Rick wriggled on his camp chair. "Is it ok to ask about the mystery animal? Are we going to try and find it today?"

"Do any of you have any ideas how to go about that?" asked Mrs. Peterson. "It's obviously very quiet and good at getting away quickly. I wonder where it hides."

"Would it be a good idea to have Clumpy look with us?" queried Cam. "I know he's a bit of a chicken and we also don't want him to scare the wildlife around here, but he might alert us to something unusual in a bush or something."

"I think that would be okay," said Talia's mother. "He might suddenly avoid a spot where an animal is hiding, so then we could carefully look in that spot. Hugh, are you in on this shadow hunt?" She smiled at her husband.

"I think I will this time." He smiled back at his wife. "As I'm sure the kids will be thinking, it's something a little different to do! Has anyone found any more feathers?"

Everyone shook their heads.

"Hmm," said Mrs. Peterson thoughtfully. "Two

mysteries, really. The owner of the shadow and the owner of the feathers. Maybe the feathers really did belong to a takahe, as we know there really are some around here."

"I guess," said Cam. He sounded disappointed.

"So, do we spread out like we did when we were looking for the glint, or what?" asked Talia.

"Well," said Mr. Peterson. "We know the shadow was here at the camp. It was over in the tree area where the loo is a couple of times. I suggest we all go to that area with the dog, and spread out a bit there, looking into all the bushes – even up into the trees. Maybe we'll find a clue."

With this goal in mind, the breakfast things were cleared away quickly. They all put on their sturdy footwear again, which was dry by now, and headed for the woods beyond the portable toilet tent.

Cassia shivered with nervous excitement. She had accepted that whatever the creature was, it didn't want to hurt any of them, but she was still uncertain what they might find! She also loved animals and didn't want anyone to frighten it or hurt it.

The campers spread out amongst the trees, using sticks to gently move leaves of bushes and shrubs aside so they could see if there was anything hiding in them. Clumpy ran around wagging his tail, seemingly oblivious to any other creature present. At one point, he growled at a bush, backing away, and Cam quietly strode over to peek into the bush. He jumped back startled when a large frog hopped out, quickly making its escape.

The Beak

As the search went on, the humans spread out further and further. There really didn't seem to be anything mysterious around at all. Even the kea had deserted them! From time to time, Mrs. Peterson's attention was caught by an unusual plant, and she resolved to come back and look at it again later.

Finally, the adults called a halt to the search. They had covered a reasonably large area in the trees beyond the campsite but had found nothing.

Belinda was glad to stop searching. "Well, that's that," she said. "Maybe it was all just a big fluke, a trick of the light."

"Or maybe it has just moved on," said Mish. "Maybe we stole its campsite and it found a new one."

Mr. Peterson chuckled. "Who's hungry? Anyone want fish pie for lunch?" He chuckled again at the non-plussed expressions around him. "I'm just kidding. There's plenty of other food still."

His wife looked thoughtful. "I've been pleased to find that we haven't seen a single rabbit or rat or stoat since we've been here," she said. "Not even a rabbit hole. Have you kids seen any?" None of them had.

"Well, that's got to be good," said Rick. "I hope they stay away! Hope none snuck here with us on the boat!" The others giggled.

"I hope not, too," said Mrs. Peterson. "We've still got a good part of the day left. If you all don't mind, I might go back to the trees after lunch and check out the flora I saw there."

"I'd love to go to the swimming hole," said Talia. "I wonder if it's still in flood? Who wants to come?"

All the other young people wanted to go. So, after the meal they once again put on their swimming things and headed for the lupin mound.

Chapter 13: Evidence

It was lovely to be walking through the tussock again in wide open space. Clumpy ran ahead while a couple of kea flew overhead, taunting him with their squawks. But they soon lost interest and flew back towards the campsite. As the young people approached the lupin mound, there was a cheerful hum of bees working busily off the flowers, and a bright chirping of smaller birds coming from the forest across the small river. A kereru suddenly flew over their heads as they reached the water hole, its wings creaking noisily.

"This is more like it," said Mish with contentment. "The waterfall is still pretty big – should be good to sit under!" With that, he threw his towel and T-shirt on the ground and made a running jump into the pool, striking out for the waterfall. The others quickly followed suit, except

Rick, who stopped to smother the exposed parts of his skin with sunscreen.

"Not taking any risks with that," he muttered to himself. Then he put his spectacles in a safe spot and jumped into the water as well.

They all had a grand time, swimming, jumping, laughing and splashing, while the sun shone down warmly. The black Labrador swam from person to person, his tongue hanging out happily.

Belinda finally emerged from the water, panting a little from her exertions. "That sun sure is nice!" she commented to the others in the pool. "Think I'll sunbathe for a while."

"We'll join you soon," said Cassia, as she and Talia floated lazily on their backs. Once again, Cassia felt grateful they had been allowed to come on such a special trip. She closed her eyes but quickly opened them again when Mish and Cam came swimming past at top speed, causing a wave that upset her delicate balance and washed over her face. "Arrgh!" moaned Cassia.

"I got to the rock first!" yelled Cam to his friend.

"It was a tie!" Mish yelled back. Then they turned again and began swimming furiously back towards the waterfall.

Meanwhile, Rick had tired of swimming and was trudging towards the rapids, which were still quite fast. He had his gold pan with him.

Belinda watched him and giggled. "You're going to try very hard to get gold while we're still here, aren't you?" She grinned at Rick.

"Sure am," he responded cheerfully. "You can have a go at it again, too, if you like, Lindy."

"Thanks, but I'm going to lie here and enjoy the sun," Belinda said, lying back on her towel. She opened one eye cautiously to check for the kereru. Didn't want another cold splash on her body!

Just then there was an exclamation from Rick. Belinda sat up again. "What is it?" she asked.

Rick held up something wet and dark. "It's a bunch of wet feathers," he said. "I think they are the same as the other ones we found. I'll let them dry out on the ground so we can get a better look."

"Okay," said Belinda. She wasn't really interested in the feathers now, as the only reasonable explanation seemed to be the takahe which weren't really too far away. Maybe one of them had gone exploring, she thought sleepily. She closed her eyes again.

After having a very satisfying time in the pool, Mish, Cam, Cassia and Talia finally climbed out of it. They dried themselves off and each found a flat, sunny spot to relax in. The afternoon sun was very pleasant.

Cam was starting to feel a bit hungry. But he didn't want to leave just yet. It was so peaceful and warm by the river, with its rippling rapids bubbling along seemingly without a care in the world. For the moment, Cam felt that he also didn't have a care in the world. He looked for Clumpy.

"You don't have a care in the world either, do you,

dog?" he said quietly, as he observed his pet. Clumpy was lying asleep on his side with hairy black legs outstretched.

Apart from the sounds of wildlife and Rick's swish, swish with his gold pan, there was silence for a while. Then Clumpy got up to find a spot to relieve himself. Having done so, he decided to venture near the waterfall to see if he could stretch out his tongue to lick the falling water.

Cassia turned her head to watch him. She was just in time to see him jump back in fright, yelping. Everyone sat up.

"What on earth is the matter, Clumpy?" said Cam crossly. "You've been there before and been swimming underneath it all morning. It's just water!"

Clumpy came running to Cam, where he stood at full alert, on the side of Cam furthest away from the pool, ears back and eyes fixed on the waterfall.

"It's probably another frog," suggested Mish, closing his eyes as he lay back down on his towel.

The three girls looked at each other. Each felt that part of her wanted to go and look at the waterfall, but another part wasn't too eager!

"Okay, who's game," said Talia finally. "He must have got frightened by something! Mum might be annoyed if we said he was startled and we didn't go to find out what."

"I'll come with you, Talia," said Cam quickly.

The two of them began walking carefully along the edge of the pool towards the waterfall, as it was still somewhat slippery after the heavy rain.

The Beak

"What's this?" said Cam suddenly. He bent down. There was another sparkly feather and two smaller red feathers. The red ones were very bright, almost scarlet.

Talia looked at the feathers. "Weird," she muttered. "We know takahe have red beaks, but I don't remember seeing any red feathers on them," she said to Cam.

"Me neither," agreed Cam. He began to have a look through the nearby lupin plants and small shrubs, hoping a sparkly bird with red feathers would pop out!

Talia looked towards the waterfall. She walked a little closer. To her, it just looked like a torrent of water falling down. Some of it splashed back on her as it hit the surface of the pool, and she jumped back. Now that she had been in the sun for a while, the splash felt very cold!

"What do you think scared Clumpy?" she asked Cam.

"I don't know," he said. "But I'll take these new feathers back to camp and see what your mum and dad think."

He and Talia turned away from the waterfall and headed back towards the others. Rick had stopped panning for gold and was coming towards them with something in his hand.

"Did you find gold?" asked Talia with interest.

"Nope," said Rick sadly. "But it's still fun trying!" His face brightened. "I found these though. They were wet when I found them, but now they are dry, I can see that they are sparkly like the others we found."

"That settles it," said Cam. "There's some kind of bird around here that is good at hiding – or doesn't happen to be here when we are. Probably a takahe, I guess. I dunno about those red feathers, though."

Belinda had been listening. She offered, "Some parrots have red feathers. There are probably some parrots around here."

"That's true," agreed Cam thoughtfully. "Hey, you two, your dad's into birds," – this directed at Mish and Rick. "So, you must know what birds might have red feathers."

A little snore came from Mish. Rick chuckled. "I hope Mish put his sunscreen on," he said. "Cam, I think there are some parrots called red-fronted parakeets, or kakariki. Mish has some photos of them from when we were across the lake at home. Maybe that's what those red feathers are? Can I see, please?"

Cam gave him a red feather. "This is quite a big feather," commented Rick. "I think the kakariki are small birds."

"We seem to be getting more bird mysteries the longer we stay here," grinned Cam.

"Well, there's nothing else to be mysterious about out here; I guess it gives the birds something to do, playing tricks on visitors," came Mish's voice from under his cap, which was now covering his face. Rick walked stealthily over to his brother. He tickled Mish's bare stomach with the red feather.

The others watched with amusement as Mish's face remained under the cap but his hand reached out to brush off whatever was on his stomach. Rick waited a moment then tickled him with the feather again. Cassia couldn't

114

help herself and exploded in a giggle. Mish lifted up his head, causing the cap to fall off. He saw his younger brother's face grinning at him while he held the feather.

"Oh, haha," he said, while the others chuckled. "Rick learned from the best, of course."

Belinda stood up and began gathering her belongings. "I don't know about you lot, but I want some food. I'm heading back to camp."

They all felt the same. Picking up their clothes and towels, they began walking towards the camp.

They had not gone very far when they heard a loud noise behind them. Everyone stopped abruptly. Clumpy barked then whined, leaning against Cam's legs.

"What was that?" asked Talia.

"It sounded like a sick goat," said Rick.

"I've never heard a sick goat before," said Mish, feigning surprise. "What do they sound like?"

"Like whatever that was," grinned Cam. "Maybe it's our mystery animal. Let's go back – might be our only chance to see it!"

"I'll stay here with Clumpy," volunteered Cassia. Belinda opted to stay with Cassia.

The rest of them returned to the pool, trying to walk as quietly as possible. The area looked the same as before. Talia glanced towards the waterfall. She peered more closely at it – she thought she had seen a movement. The water continued to fall in torrents. She quickly concluded it was just the falling stream she had noticed.

"Can't see anything here," said Mish. "Perhaps it was yet another kind of bird. Maybe one no one has discovered yet and it's sitting across in those trees laughing at us." He gestured towards the forest on the other side of the small river.

"Wouldn't surprise me," agreed Cam. "Anyway, now I'm *really* hungry. Let's go!"

The four of them caught up to Cassia, Belinda and Clumpy.

"Nothing to report," said Rick. "Mish thinks it might have been an undiscovered bird in the trees across from the river."

"Hmm," said Belinda.

"Perhaps the wild animals have become so used to us being here that they're all coming out to play," suggested Talia.

"Well, they've only got a few days left to get to know us," said Cam with a laugh. "I can feel my tummy rumbling. Let's get back to camp."

Upon arrival at the campsite, they were all pleased to see the array of food laid out on the fold-up table – potato chips with dip, apples, cheese and crackers, and tinned baby beetroots.

"Tomatoes would have been nice with the cheese and crackers," commented Mr. Peterson. "But we finished them all."

"Interesting lot of food," observed his wife. "But I guess we're getting down to whatever was long life or could be kept cold. Not keen on this powdered milk, though!" She grimaced as she sipped her tea.

"We found more feathers!" burst out Rick. "Red ones! And we heard a weird noise. But we couldn't find what was making the noise."

"May I see the red feathers, please?" asked Mrs. Peterson with interest. Cam passed over his feathers.

"Here's the other ones I found today, wet from the stream where I was panning for gold," added Rick. He handed them to Mrs. Peterson.

She compared all the feathers then put them down. "You know what, I think these are from the same creature. Although the colours and sizes are different, they are very similar in other respects. I don't think takahe have red feathers like this, though. This mystery bird is quite tantalizing! I'm not yet convinced it's a moa, though, Cam." She grinned at him. He smiled back at her.

"Well, it's something," said her husband, getting up to refill their water boiling pot and knocking a teaspoon onto the ground as he did so. "I need another cup of coffee. Hey, you! Bring that spoon back!" A pesky kea had swooped near his foot and grabbed the teaspoon.

Clumpy jumped up, ready to run and hide. As usual, when the kea opened its beak to caw at the dog, the teaspoon fell to the ground.

"We need to be careful not to let those birds get any of our utensils," warned Mrs. Peterson, retrieving the teaspoon. "We really want to leave this place as pristine as when we found it."

"We've just got to convince the kea of that," said her husband with a grin.

Chapter 14: Night Visitor

The next two days passed uneventfully. The weather remained fine. Everyone spent some time at the edge of the sound fishing, and they also all went on another hike to see the newly discovered takahe flock, taking lots of photos. There was no flooded river on the way back this time. The adults found time to swim in the pool below the waterfall. No more sparkly feathers were found, but the group did swim to the other side of the pool and explore a little of the forest, noting the many varieties of native birds residing there. Kereru were plentiful, often startling them with a sudden creaky whoosh as they flew overhead.

"Have you noticed that the kea don't come over here?" Talia asked her mother on one of these occasions. "It's not far for them to go and I would have thought they might follow us, since they seem to like hanging around people."

"Perhaps their nest area is close to where we are," her mother responded. "But you're right – they could fly here and back to the campsite very quickly."

"Maybe they're in a feud with the forest birds here," said Mish. "A pecking war."

"Humph," said Talia, rolling her eyes.

"I'm going to miss this place," commented Belinda sadly. "It's been so peaceful. No cars, no social media! Just beautiful nature and rest."

"No little sisters either," Cassia teased her friend.

"Actually, I miss Mum and Jackie," confessed Belinda. "I think every day I've seen something or done something that I wanted to share with them."

"I haven't had that problem," grinned Mish. He looked at his younger brother, who even at that moment had his gold pan out again and was entrenched between a couple of rocks downstream from the pool. Mish called out to him.

"Rick! Have you found any gold at all on this trip?"

Rick turned his head slightly and nodded.

"Don't you remember, Mish?" Belinda put in. "He got that tiny dot in the stream beside the camp when I was doing it, too."

"Oh, right," said Mish. "Is your gold panning better than his, then, Lindy?"

Belinda laughed. "I doubt it. But it is fun, and I can see why lots of adults just want to keep doing it and doing it, hoping for that big nugget!"

120

"Indeed," said Mrs. Peterson. "Gold fever, they call it. Let's hope Rick doesn't get it. At least not till he's old enough to really do something with it."

"Oh, Rick will probably end up being a famous scientist or an engineer, or something like that," remarked Mish airily.

"Yes, he's very clever," agreed Belinda.

Mrs. Peterson smiled. "I seem to recall that you did very well at school this past year as well, Lindy. A clever bunch, you lot are! Eek!"

Her husband had just swum quietly to the edge of the pool behind her and splashed her. "Want to come in again, sweetheart? It might be the last time!"

Mrs. Peterson nodded and let herself down into the pool daintily. Soon she and her husband were slowly swimming in sidestroke around the pool.

The whole lot of them were tired that night after dinner. "Great job with the fish pancakes, Cam," Cassia complimented her brother. "You'll have to make them for Mum and Dad at home!"

"Not for a while!" he laughed. "I love fishing but eating fish all the time is not as much fun as I thought it would be."

They all turned in early. Sometimes they had found it hard to get to sleep because it stayed light outside until very late, but they were so worn out with swimming and hiking that it wasn't long before they were all asleep.

Cassia woke suddenly in the night. It was a bright night,

with a full moon, causing tree shadows to be easily seen against the side of the tent. Cassia looked at her watch then stayed very still. There was a shadow outside the tent which she was sure was *not* a tree. It moved past the tent in an unhurried manner. It was quite tall, and like Cam, Cassia felt there was something beak-like about the upper part of it.

Cassia could not bring herself to move. Even though they had all concluded that the owner of the shadow was harmless, it was disconcerting to have it right outside her tent in the middle of the night. She was too scared to even nudge the other girls, who were sleeping peacefully. She lay like a statue. The shadow moved on, disappearing from her sight. She had not heard any footsteps, but as it moved away, there was an odd sound – like a quieter version of what they had heard a couple of days before at the pool.

Talia stirred. Cassia found her voice. "Talia!" she hissed. "Wake up! The shadow is back! And it made a noise!"

Talia struggled to open her eyes. "Shadows make noise?" she slurred sleepily. Waking properly, she realized what Cassia was saying. "The shadow is here?" she said more loudly, sitting up.

Belinda woke up. "What's going on?" she asked, seeing the two girls sitting up.

"Cassia said the shadow is back and it made a noise," said Talia.

"Ooh!" said Belinda. "Time for us to be brave! And where's Clumpy when you need him?"

That made Cassia smile. "I think the three of us are all braver than my dog. Okay then, let's go find out what this mysterious creature is." Just as she said it, they heard the odd sound again. It sounded as though it was between their tent and Talia's parents' tent.

Cassia could not bring herself to move.

A moment later, they heard Mr. Peterson calling out. "Are you kids okay? Did you hear anything?"

Cassia saw the light of a lantern through the tent wall, so she felt it would be safe enough to put on her dressing gown and go outside. The other two girls did the same and soon the three of them were standing with Mr. and Mrs. Peterson under the big tent's awning. Moths swarmed around the little lantern.

"We heard a weird scream," said Mrs. Peterson. "We were worried it was one of you."

"It sounded like a goat," said Mr. Peterson.

"A sick one?" grinned Talia. "We heard that, too, a few days ago by the pool."

"Whatever it is, it's getting bolder," said her father.

Cassia looked over towards the trees by the toilet tent. She didn't really want to use it during the night if there were going to be shadowy, screeching goat-creatures sneaking around!

"I don't think it's out to do any harm," said Mrs. Peterson, as if she had read Cassia's thoughts. "More likely it has realized we are not going to do it any harm and it's curious. We are in its territory, after all."

"It would be helpful to know exactly what *it* is, Mum," countered Talia.

"I'll go and have yet another scout around the trees," said Mr. Peterson. He gave the lantern to his wife to hold.

"Oh, Dad, don't you want to take the light with you?" asked Talia.

"No," he replied. "It's a moonlit night, and I'm more likely to scare the creature off if I come barging through the trees with a light. Wait here, everyone, and if anything makes a run for you, get inside the tent and zip up the door!" With that cheerful suggestion, he was off, striding silently across the grass towards the trees.

Belinda shivered as she stood there. "I'm surprised Clumpy isn't making a noise, and the boys are still asleep."

"Most likely Clumpy has huddled up to Cam," responded Cassia. "I guess the boys were pretty tired after all their swimming races yesterday."

The four of them waited patiently for Mr. Peterson to return. He did finally, only to report that while he thought he had seen a movement further into the trees, he was not able to catch up to it. "I didn't really want to trip on something and go sprawling," he said. "I think it's gone home now anyway, wherever home is."

"Maybe *this* is home, and we are in it," said Cassia.

"Maybe," said Mrs. Peterson. "But unlikely, I think, as most of the feathers have been found nearer the river where the waterfall is. It must have a good hide-out, though! And I wonder if there is only one – we only seem to see one shadow!"

"Unless they take turns – like soldiers on patrol," said Talia.

"Really," giggled Cassia. She felt better now that Mr. Peterson was back.

"Well, I'm going back to bed," said Mrs. Peterson. "We only have one more day here before the boat comes to get us the following morning – let's make it count!"

The little group dispersed, the girls returning to their tent where they soon fell asleep again once snuggled back into their sleeping bags.

The three girls slept late in the morning. Cassia woke up to Clumpy licking her face. Cam had unzipped the tent door and was looking in. "Are you all still asleep?" he said in a surprised tone. "Last day here today! Poached eggs and fish for breakfast!"

Talia groaned and turned over. Then she came wide awake. "Cam! Did you hear us all in the night?"

"Hear what?" Cam paused.

"The shadow came back during the night and made that sick goat sound at us. It woke Mum and Dad, too."

Mish's face appeared beside Cam. "Wh-a-at?" he said indignantly. "You saw the shadow and didn't wake us?"

Cassia answered him. "It was a bit nerve-wracking. I saw it first but was too scared to move or say anything. It was only when Talia woke that I told her, then we heard it out in the camp area. It was like that noise we heard by the pool when we were leaving the other day."

"Leave us to get dressed, and we'll be out shortly and tell you all about it over breakfast." said Belinda, climbing out of her sleeping bag. "I'm looking forward to poached eggs! I might skip the fish, though."

Soon everyone was seated around the fold-up table eating breakfast. There was excited talk as the girls explained to the boys what had taken place during the night. Cam was most disappointed.

"I wish you had wakened us," he said. "Our only chance to go chasing the shadow to find out what it was!"

"You might have frightened it if you had done that," his sister reminded him. "What about Clumpy? Didn't you notice him whine or anything in the night, Cam?"

Cam shook his head. "When I woke up, Clumpy was

126

just about in my sleeping bag with me. But he seemed quite happy about that."

"I slept right through it all, too," moaned Rick. "Why didn't the shadow come by *my* tent?"

"Maybe it did and you slept right through it," suggested Belinda.

"Anyone want more eggs and fish?" asked Mr. Peterson, coming up just then with a full pan of steaming food.

"I will, thanks," said Rick. Mr. Peterson used a spatula to put some fish and an egg on Rick's plate. The other children politely turned down the offer of more food.

Mrs. Peterson had been sitting in a camp chair quietly sipping her tea. Now she spoke. "We will probably have to leave without having solved the mystery of this beaked creature that makes a noise like a sick goat. Today we need to get everything packed up and organized ready for the tents to be taken down in the morning. I expect Captain Rod to arrive about morning teatime and he will not be wanting to stay here long, so we need to be ready to load it at the rocks."

"Yes, the trip back will take a few hours like it did last time," said her husband. "I imagine the captain would want to get back by late afternoon."

Belinda sighed. "A hot shower. Loving the thought!"

"Sausage rolls and pies!" said Rick.

"A new pillow for Christmas!" Mish taunted Cam.

"Fresh normal milk out of a bottle," laughed Mrs.

127

Peterson. "Actually, I'm looking forward to a hot shower, too. Treading water under a steady waterfall has been lovely, but it's not quite the same!"

"Wow!" said Cassia suddenly. "It'll be Christmas when we get back! I've hardly thought about it here – we are so far away from the bustle of everything."

"There's not much time to do shopping," observed Mr. Peterson.

"We all did it before we left," responded Cam. "But if Mish wants to buy me a new pillow, I'll take it!"

"Maybe the shadow will try to stop us getting back on the boat," said Mish. "Maybe it wants to have Christmas with us!"

Cassia and Belinda looked alarmed at this thought, but Talia laughed good-naturedly, although she did glance towards the trees. "Oh, haha, Mish," she said.

Cam threw a tea towel at Mish. "I think the shadow wants you to wash and dry the dishes!"

Chapter 15: The Last Night

They spent the day packing up, only leaving out the bare essentials. Belinda glanced at the sky a few times. Now and then grey clouds scudded across it.

At afternoon teatime, she spoke to Mr. and Mrs. Peterson. "What happens if the weather gets bad and the boat gets into trouble on the way?"

"That's unlikely," she was reassured. "If the forecast looks poor, the captain won't come till the weather improves, and we have enough to get by with for a few more days if necessary. But the long-range forecast was for mild weather."

By the evening, the clouds had passed. The sky was beautiful and clear, with a soft blue hue. The campers sat on the rocks at the shore for a while, enjoying the quietness of the sounds, the towering mountains and sleepy birdsong. Now and then, there was a flapping as a seal slid off a rock on the other side of the sound. The sun lowered, casting a faint orange hue over the beautiful panorama. Everyone was silent, once again aware of the remoteness of their location, barely touched by humans, almost primeval. Even Clumpy lay quiet and still.

Presently, Mr. Peterson said, "I do believe that on a night like this we may see an aurora. We're far enough south that we could."

"Is that when the sky changes to green?" queried Belinda.

"Yes," answered Mrs. Peterson. "Does anyone know what causes that?"

Rick answered. "It's because of charged particles from the sun, like when there's a solar storm interacting with the earth's magnetic field, isn't it?"

"That's right, Rick," she smiled. "Auroras typically occur at the very north of the planet and at the very south. Sometimes they look like big green curtains hanging in the sky."

"I'd love to see that!" cried Belinda enthusiastically.

"Me, too," echoed the others.

"Well, let's go and have a hot chocolate with marshmallows then come back a bit later," said Mr. Peterson.

"Yum! Come on, Clumpy!" said Cam. He and the black dog walked briskly back to the campsite while everyone else followed.

The Beak

"Hope you didn't pack up the marshmallows, Rick," Mish said as an aside to his brother.

"As if," retorted Rick. "Hope *you* are looking forward to your fried fish in the morning!" Mish laughed.

The campers talked very little as they sipped their hot chocolates. Clumpy munched contentedly on a dog biscuit. The kea were nowhere to be seen. Nor was the shadow. As the evening wore on, the southern sky took on a blue-yellow tinge, gradually becoming light green. Twinkling pinpricks of stars appeared in the night sky.

"Oh, is that it?" asked Talia excitedly.

"Yes," said Mr. Peterson. "Would you all like to go back to the shore? We can see it quite well from here."

"I'd love to go back to the shore," said Belinda. "Our last night here!"

Everyone agreed, so they rinsed and put away their cups then trooped back to the rocks at the edge of the sound. There were different noises now – low rustlings in the trees and shrubs nearby, causing Clumpy to growl a little. He was startled as a large moth flew right past his nose. As usual, he stayed close to Cam's legs.

Soon they were all seated, as comfortably as one could be on a rock, to watch the night sky unfold. The light green hue deepened to grass green with streaks of pink and yellow.

"It's like a rainbow sky," commented Cassia.

"Beautiful," breathed Belinda.

Even Mish was more serious than usual, gazing with

spellbound eyes at the magnificent vista of sky and stars.

The group sat there for a while, until Rick suddenly gave a huge yawn.

"Time for bed, I think," remarked Mrs. Peterson. "It's been beautiful – but I'm about ready to hit the pillow as well!"

As the evening wore on, the southern sky took on a blue-yellow tinge, gradually becoming light green. Twinkling pinpricks of stars appeared in the night sky.

Slowly the two adults and six young people made their way back to the camp. Although no one said anything, each of them felt a little sad that this would be their last night at the lovely isolated spot.

The Beak

As Rick prepared to close the zip of his tent door, he called to the other boys. "Do you think the shadow will come back tonight? Maybe we should wait up and see?"

Mish laughed from the blue dome tent. "Well, you can try if you want, bro, but I'd be surprised if you managed to stay awake for that. Do you want Clumpy in there with you?"

"No, thanks," said Rick. "There's only just enough room for me, I've decided. Well, goodnight then!" He waited for Mish to say goodnight then zipped up his door. Snuggling down into his sleeping bag, he really did intend to lie awake in case the shadow came. A slight wind sprang up, causing the branches of the big bush next to his tent to move in the breeze. They produced shadows which moved back and forth hypnotically. Rick watched carefully to see if one looked as though it had a beak, but before long, he was fast asleep.

Chapter 16: Beyond the Waters

There were no disturbances that night. The little camp lay silent and peaceful as the sun rose in the east, causing the slightly rippling water in the nearby stream to glisten.

The kea woke everyone very early. Someone had dropped a teaspoon the night before without noticing, and now two of the birds were fighting over it.

Cam stretched out his arms. He gave Clumpy a pat and unzipped the door for him. The black Labrador quickly headed towards a tree, hoping the squabbling kea didn't notice him. Both kea rose into the air crossly. One held the teaspoon in its beak. It caught sight of Clumpy trying to hide behind the tree and flew over, opening its beak to scold the dog. The teaspoon fell, hitting Clumpy on the nose. He yelped in surprise. What weapon did those noisy birds have now?

The Beak

Cam had come out of the tent to watch the interaction between Clumpy and the kea. He couldn't help laughing. Mish and Rick put their heads out of their tents at the same moment.

"What's so funny?" asked Mish.

"Just Clumpy and those birds," said Cam. "One of them dropped a spoon on his nose."

"Ooh, grab the spoon fast," called Talia from her tent.

Cam picked up the teaspoon, taking it over to the breakfast table. Then he looked at the table regretfully. This was the last time it would be used on this trip.

"I wonder if we'll ever get to come here again, Talia," he said, as she walked up behind him.

"Yeah, I know," she said. "It's almost like a once-in-a-lifetime thing."

By this time, nearly everyone else was dressed. The cheerful hiss of the gas stove with water boiling in a pot filled the morning air – but there was no fish!

"What happened, Dad?" asked Talia, giggling a little. "Did we actually run out of fish?"

Her father grinned at her. "Your mother and I saved a little surprise for last." He brandished a packet. "Pancake mix! With maple syrup. Perhaps then you'll think of your fish meals with nostalgia in future."

"Yummy!" said Rick. "Can I help, please?"

"Sure," said Mr. Peterson. Soon the two of them were whipping up the pancake mix in a bowl, using the remainder of the powdered milk, and frying portions of the mixture in the pan on the little stove. The aroma was delicious. Maple syrup was poured over the cooked pancakes. Everyone ate at least two and enjoyed them heartily.

After breakfast, they had to do the final pack down. The bedding was rolled up and stacked in bundles, and the tents taken down, brushed and folded back into their storage bags. All the young people pitched in to wipe down the table, wash and pack dishes and food. They were careful to make sure they collected every bit of rubbish to take back with them in a big bag. Then all the gear was carried to the shore, to the flat rocks at which they had first landed. Because they had done most of the packing the day before, and had woken so early, it was still well before morning tea when they were finished.

Belinda stared out along the water, waiting for a glimpse of the fishing boat.

Mr. Peterson noticed her looking and said, "It will be mid to late morning before they are here, I would think. It's a beautiful day, though, so the boat will come."

"Perhaps you would all like to go for a walk to the waterfall," suggested his wife. "There is plenty of time. Just don't go swimming, because we don't want to have to deal with wet clothes or towels at this stage."

"Great idea," enthused Mish. "Coming, kids?"

"Yes, Dad," said Cam, saluting his friend.

The six friends and the dog left the adults sitting on the rocks and began the leisurely hike over the expanse of tussock towards the river. As they drew near, they could hear the rapids bubbling over the rocks as the water flowed downstream. The sun shone brightly.

"There's some heat in that sun," commented Mish. "I'd almost like to go for a last swim!"

"Better not, though," advised Talia. "Wet clothes might not seem a problem here, but once you're out on the open sea, it might be a bit chilly and unpleasant to be in them. And no one wants to have to carry wet clothes around."

"Good point," acknowledged Mish. He suddenly remembered his seasickness of the trip up the coast and grimaced. "I hope I don't get seasick today."

"Me neither," agreed Rick.

Belinda walked over to the lupin mound to admire the blooms. "So pretty," she said.

"We do get lupins closer to home, you know," Talia told her. "So it's not the last time you'll see them!"

"I wonder how Toto is," Rick pondered aloud.

"The cousins will probably be glad to hand him back," said Mish.

The young people sat along the edge of the pool for a while, listening to the sound of the falling water for the last time. There seemed to be more wood pigeons around than usual, flying back and forth over the pool.

"I wonder if they know we're leaving," said Belinda.

"Do you really think it was a wood pigeon that plopped water on your back that time?" Cassia giggled.

Belinda laughed, too. "I don't know. I don't know what

else it could have been. Unless it was one of you being sneaky."

"Listen!" exclaimed Cam.

"What?" said the others together. They all paused for a moment to listen. Then they heard what Cam had heard – the far-off chug of an engine.

"It's the fishing boat," said Talia.

"It's so quiet here that the sound carries a long way," observed Cam. "And maybe the high mountains in the fjord make it echo a bit."

"I guess that means we'd better make our way back," said Mish.

"Well, goodbye, waterfall, river, lupins and all you birdies," said Belinda, waving at the vista before her. "Merry Christmas!"

All the children gazed around at the beautiful spot once more. Then they began to make their way back to the campsite, with Mish and Cam in the lead. Cassia turned her head to watch Clumpy as he trotted over to the water's edge, lowering his head to lap the pool water. He paused, raising his head towards the waterfall. Then instead of joining the children, he began walking away from them, along the edge of the pool towards the waterfall.

"Clumpy!" Cassia called crossly.

Cam turned to see what the dog was doing, whistling for him. Clumpy wagged his tail but kept going towards the waterfall. Cam sighed.

"Cam, you keep going," said Cassia. "I'll fetch Clumpy

and catch up." Her brother nodded and turned back to the others.

Cassia quickly ran after the black dog. Just as he reached the side of the waterfall, he slipped with a yelp, going into the water and disappearing under the falling stream.

"Oh, Clumpy!" Cassia said again. "I am *not* going to come into that water and get you! Come here!" To her surprise, the dog didn't reappear, and she called him again. Then she heard a whine. It sounded as though he was in the waterfall!

"Where are you, boy?" she said loudly. The only response was another whine.

"Clumpy?" she called tentatively. A deep bark sounded then another whine. She moved closer to the side of the waterfall, looking down at the ground to check her footing. Cautiously, Cassia edged closer to the falling water, trying to avoid the fine spray that flicked roguishly off to the side. She realized there was a small gap between the falling water and the cliff behind it.

"Clumpy!" she muttered again. Cassia sighed and poked her head through the gap behind the water, trying not to get too wet. She saw then that just past the outermost part of the falling stream, there was a ledge wide enough to walk on sideways, with the water falling in front of it. If she was careful, she might be able to step through the thin outermost stream to get to the ledge. This she managed successfully, then paused to take stock of the situation. The ledge appeared to go part way along the width of the cliff face behind the waterfall. She was able to sidle along it fairly easily. To Cassia's surprise, she found there was a narrow recess behind the waterfall, like a small but tall cave, which was where Clumpy now stood, looking back at the water. He trotted up to Cassia, licked her hand, then shook himself, shaking water all over Cassia.

"Arrgh. Okay, boy, you got in here. So, you must be able to get out," she told the black dog. Cassia looked into the recess. "What a pity we didn't discover this while we were swimming," she murmured to herself. "We could have had heaps of fun with it! Come on, Clumpy! We have to go – the boat's nearly here." She moved towards the ledge. Not wanting to be left alone behind the waterfall again, Clumpy took an eager leap past her, scraping clumsily along the ledge, back out to the sunshine. Cassia could vaguely see him through the falling water, looking back at her with his tongue hanging out. He seemed quite happy now.

There was a yell from a distance and Clumpy turned and disappeared from view, in the direction of the voice.

For a few moments, Cassia stood behind the waterfall, admiring the iridescent effect of the sunshine on the falling stream, like rainbow colours through a prism. She was about to make her own way back along the ledge, when she turned her head for one final look at the recess – and found herself looking straight into the eyes of a very tall bird. It was standing only a short distance away. Cassia sucked in her breath, stopping herself from crying out in fright. She remained quite still, looking at the creature. Its beak was large, red and about level with her nose. The neck was long and graceful. Its legs, which were also long, but thick and sturdy-looking, were as red as its beak. The bird was as tall as she was. But it was the plumage that really caught her attention. The large torso was covered in purplish-blue feathers which variegated to violet and dark blue on its back. As the sunshine glinted through the waterfall it seemed that the feathers sparkled and glittered.

Cassia again stopped herself from gasping out loud. The creature was beautiful. The bird looked back at her, apparently curious but only a little cautious. Its eyes were black with red outer rings.

"You're very fast and stealthy," she told it softly. "Was it you making those goat noises then, and lurking around our tents?"

The bird stared back at her without answering.

Cassia watched it, thinking how exciting it would be to tell everyone she had solved the mystery of the elusive shadow. Then she remembered how people could destroy lovely discoveries. This bird and its family – if it had one – had existed here peacefully for hundreds of years, most likely. Already the public were going to hear about the newly found flock of takahe birds.

Just then Cassia heard the faint sound of a shout and involuntarily looked behind her. When she turned back to the bird, it was in time to see a pert, red, stumpy tail feather disappearing into what must be a cleft in the rock further back in the recess. Cassia hesitated. Then she turned and made her way outside. The sound of her name was becoming louder and nearer. Cam appeared from around the lupin mound.

"Cassia!" he called. "Come on – Clumpy's with me."

"Okay, coming!" she called back. She knelt to retie her shoelace as Cam disappeared around the mound. Cassia stood up and looked back at the waterfall. Again, she felt as if she was being watched. But it no longer bothered her.

"Your secret's safe with me," she whispered.

About the author: Sherri Bee lives in New Zealand. She has a large family, scattered around Australasia. She loves children and animals and usually has several cats! Her house has a lagoon on one side and a beach a short walk away on the other. Sherri likes to have fun and people who stay at her house have been known to be startled by a squeaky toy hidden under their pillow!

www.ingramcontent.com/pod-product-compliance
Lightning Source LLC
LaVergne TN
LVHW011354080426
835511LV00005B/292